Another Spanner in the Works

Challenging prejudice and racism in mainly white schools

Eleanor Knowles and Wendy Ridley

Trentham Books
Stoke on Trent, UK and Sterling, USA

Trentham Books Limited

Westview House   22883 Quicksilver Drive
734 London Road   Sterling
Oakhill   VA 20166-2012
Stoke on Trent   USA
Staffordshire
England ST4 5NP

© 2005 Eleanor Knowles and Wendy Ridley

First published 2006

British Library Cataloguing-in-Publication Data
A catalogue record for this book is available from the British Library

ISBN-13: 978-1-85856-347-3
ISBN-10: 1-85856-347-X

Designed and typeset by Trentham Print Design Ltd, Chester and printed in Great Britain by Bemrose Shafron (Printers) Ltd, Chester

Contents

Section 1 – What do we do about entrenched attitudes?

1.1: I live here and I think ... perceptions of a locality • 4

1.2: Perceptions of a contrasting locality within a region • 5

1.3: Perceptions of Britain – a diverse society • 7

1.4: All about me ... exploring my own identity • 10

1.5: I am a Cumbrian and who are you? • 11

1.6: Finding out about me • 14

1.7: Baseline assessment • 16

Section 2 – How do we embed equality in whole-school practice?

2.1: Whole-school approach ... starting from a Healthy Schools Policy • 20

2.2: Whole-school approach ... based on progression through the school • 24

2.3: Whole-school approach ... through an underlying curriculum • 27

2.4: Whole-school approach ... through multi-school art projects • 31

2.5: Whole-school approach ... involving the whole school community • 33

Section 3 – How do we build on community issues and school situations?

3.1: Dealing with racist incidents • 38

3.2: Responding during circle time to a racist incident • 41

3.3: Supporting a non-English speaker in school • 42

3.4: *Keeping Diversity on Track* • 46

3.5: Extending an overseas student's contribution across the school • 48

3.6: Supporting Traveller pupils in the classroom • 50

3.7: Including Traveller culture in the curriculum • 52

3.8: Responding to negative attitudes towards Islam • 55

3.9: Adapting antiracist education activities for pupils with special educational needs • 56

Section 4 – What teaching and learning strategies are effective?

4.1: *Ally Comes to Cumbria* – an anti-racist forum theatre production • 58

4.2: *Escape to Safety* – interactive exhibition on refugees • 60

4.3: Philosophical enquiry and Philosophy for Children • 63

4.4: Building on philosophical enquiry to tackle antiracist education • 66

4.5: An enquiry approach at Foundation Stage • 69

4.6: An overview of school linking • 71

4.7: School linking visits within the local community • 73

4.8: Persona dolls • 74

4.9: Working with a class mascot to support multicultural education • 77

4.10: Using a resources box for multicultural education • 80

Section 5 – How do we evaluate and reflect? How do we move on from just celebrating cultures?

5.1: Evaluating classroom practice and whole school approaches • 86

5.2: We're doing a week about ... guidelines on culture weeks • 88

5.3: Using books in antiracist and multicultural education • 92

5.4: Using artefacts from other cultures and places • 93

5.5: Using images of other cultures and places • 95

5.6: Contacts and Resources • 99

Acknowledgements

This book relied on the willing participation and expertise of:

Alison Wilde, Tebay Community Primary School, Tebay

Alison Williams, St Gregory and St Patrick's Catholic Infant School, Whitehaven

Carly Dodd, Heron Hill Primary School, Kendal

Caroline Fanshawe, Braithwaite CE Primary School, near Keswick

Chrissie Clark, Harrington Infant School (now Beckstone Primary School), Workington

Christian Robertson, Belah School, Carlisle

Colin Smith, Greengate Junior School, Barrow

Deborah Hope, Caldew Lea School, Carlisle

Karen Stringer, St George's CE School. Barrow

Gill Harris, Fairfield Infant School, Cockermouth

Helen Dixon, Kendal Nursery School, Kendal

Helen Wheatley, Appleby Primary School

Jackie Chambers, Ambleside CE Primary School

Jan Ashbridge, St Mary's CE Primary School, Kirkby Lonsdale

Jane Nattrass, Long Marton Community Primary School, near Appleby

Jenny Boothman, Pennington CE School

Jenny Dixon, Armathwaite School, near Penrith

Judith Gore, St Mary's CE Nursery and Infant School, Windermere

Pauline Robertson and Kath Hodgson, Victoria Infant and Nursery School, Workington

Katy Palmer, Sedbergh Primary School

Lindsay Ferrie, Grasmere CE School

Louisa Day, Specialist Advisory Teaching Service

Lucy McCullough and Carys Munnoch, Petteril Bank Primary School, Carlisle

Mark Squires, Langdale CE Primary School

Peggy Turner, Sandside Lodge School, Ulverston

Philippa Hartley, Thwaites School

Sara Wilson, Sandgate School, Kendal

Staff of Appleby Primary School

Staff of St Cuthbert's Catholic Primary School, Wigton

Staff of St Michaels Infant and Nursery School, Workington

Sue Bone, High Hesket CE School, near Carlisle

Veronica Creswell, Lamplugh CE School

We'd like to thank them all.

We could not have produced this book without the ideas, enthusiasm and commitment of colleagues at Cumbria Development Education Centre and at Cumbria Education Service.

We are particularly indebted to Jane Yates whose work at CDEC and as an advisory teacher has informed the practice of many schools in Cumbria, and who conceived, designed or carried out some of the projects featured in this book. Indeed, were it not for her maternity leave, she would have been part of the author team.

We also wish to thank Gina Mullarkey, Vimala John, Lesley Hagon and Gisela Renolds whose tireless energy and high quality practice and support for schools has furthered the work of antiracist and multicultural education in Cumbria in many ways. Their work is also featured in this book.

This book would not have been written without the energy and vision of the authors of the original *Spanner in the Works* (Clare Brown, Jacqui Barnfield and Mary Stone). We also thank our editor at Trentham Books, Gillian Klein, who has supported this project from the beginning.

Finally, the day-to-day encouragement of Arthur Capstick at CDEC and our families at home (Paul and the children and Steve) has ensured that we did, at last, reach the end.

Terms and abbreviations

Advisory teacher
Reference to an advisory teacher throughout the book refers to members of the team of *Advisory Teachers for Multicultural and Antiracist Education*, part of Cumbria Education Service

CDEC
Cumbria Development Education Centre

P4C
Philosophy for Children

Parents
Any reference to parents in the book also includes carers

All personal names uswd within the text are fictitious.

Preface

This book is about moving on. In the first instance it is an attempt to move on from *Spanner in the Works*, published in 1990, which described over 30 projects tackling education for racial equality and social justice in white schools in Cumbria. Since then much has changed: in the school curriculum, in widespread understanding about the need for, and the challenge of, antiracist education, and in the increased suspicion and hostility among different cultures around the world. But there has also been some progress, notably the strengthening of race relations legislation that came into effect in 2002.

It is a requirement of the Race Relations (Amendment) Act (2000) that all public bodies, including schools, have a duty, in everything that they do, to:

- eliminate unlawful racial discrimination

- promote equality of opportunity

- promote good race relations between people of different racial, ethnic and religious groups

Schools have a specific duty to:

- prepare and maintain a written race equality policy

- reassess and monitor the impact of policies on pupils, parents and staff from different racial groups

- where reasonably practical, to publish the results of monitoring and assessments

Schools in predominantly white communities often find it a challenge to make the race equality agenda real for their pupils. Some schools underplay the significance of race equality issues because they have few, if any, ethnic minority pupils. But mainstreaming race equality is essential. The duty to promote good race relations applies to every individual in every school because it is about preparing pupils to live harmoniously in the multi-ethnic society of which we are all part. This is not about being politically correct, it is about justice and fairness for all groups and protecting the rights of everyone. That includes noticing similarities as well as celebrating differences. Many mainly white schools want to celebrate diversity as the norm, but are unsure how to acknowledge the existence of prejudice.

Teachers in mainly white schools often say that they have more pressing equality issues relating to gender, homophobia, special educational needs and disability.

They are unsure how to apply their learning to other marginalised groups so that every group counts and there is no hierarchy of acceptance.

This book is also about moving on in another sense: from the starting point of multicultural activities and celebrating other cultures, to tackling hard issues of negative perceptions, intolerance and prejudice.

Race equality planning must be more than just a paper exercise. It should help ensure that race equality concerns are integrated into all aspects of school life, with an action plan focusing on the outcomes for pupils of implementing the race equality policy and clear links into the school improvement plan and school self evaluation process.

Monitoring the policy should be a regular item at governors' meetings as the governors are responsible for ensuring that the school fulfils its responsibilities under the Race Relations Amendment Act.

A race equality action plan should give the school an opportunity to review and evaluate what it has been doing and to move forward in a more systematic way.

The projects and activities described in this book are based on principles of respect and acceptance. They are not about celebrating other people and cultures as an end in itself, but about identifying, reflecting on and challenging attitudes to other groups whom we perceive as different, and developing our ability to question what we have learned, or have been told, about the out-group.

The task for schools is complex. Children come to school with pre-formed attitudes, influenced by their parents, their grandparents, the media and the attitudes and cultural values held by their community. The challenge is to tackle the range of attitudes that pervade the whole school, including the staff and the wider community. In any community there will be some minority groups and incomers (or 'off-comers' as they are called in Cumbria) who are considered 'safe' to learn about, and others who are virtually taboo. These might not, at first glance, be associated with racism. They might be incomers of many kinds, from Gypsies and Travellers to refugees and asylum-seekers to second-home owners or people from a different estate. Challenging local 'tribalism' is part of the race equality agenda.

> Having the Traveller home corner in Reception class was fine. None of the parents were worried by that. We don't see any Travellers here, so it is a neutral issue.

But a holiday cottage home corner – that would be overstepping the line; I don't think I could do it. About 70% of the houses in this village are holiday homes and there is great bitterness locally about the people who buy these houses.
> *Cumbrian primary school headteacher*

In Cumbria there has been a significant drive to tackle attitudes and racism in the fifteen years since *Spanner in the Works* appeared. Cumbria Development Education Centre (CDEC) has grown from its small beginnings before 1990 to become a county-wide organisation working with a range of schools and community groups on issues at the heart of the global, multicultural and antiracist agenda. Many of the activities in this book have been inspired and supported by CDEC. CDEC's influence is particularly strong in school linking projects, in the use of philosophical enquiry and Philosophy for Children, and in using images and overseas artefacts to challenge perceptions of people and places. And some schools are still successfully building on the activities and programmes which featured in the original *Spanner in the Works*.

Equally significant, Cumbria Education Service has advisory teachers for antiracist and multicultural education working alongside advisory teachers for Travellers and for English as an additional language. Many schools across Cumbria have received training in race equality approaches, involving teachers, teaching assistants, governors, midday supervisors and, in some cases, parents. Major educational programmes such as provision for English as a supplementary language; work with Travellers; forum theatre (*Ally Comes to Cumbria and Just Passing*); interactive exhibitions (*Escape to Safety* and *Fortress Europe*), the use of persona dolls and Philosophy for Children have been developed. Grants from Cumbria Education Service have supported school projects relating to race equality, some of them described here. This book reflects the strong and long-standing working partnership between CDEC and Cumbria Education Service.

Changes in the political, social and educational climate mean that children are generally more in touch with the wider world than fifteen years ago, for example being streetwise in their own community and likely to travel overseas or communicate through the internet. However, there is also greater external pressure to incite hatred of others, not least as a result of 9/11, the London bombings and other terrorist activities. While this book highlights some good practice in Cumbria, it is hard to imagine a time when the job of antiracist education will be complete.

What do we do about entrenched attitudes?

The number of black and ethnic minority people living in Cumbria is relatively small – 0.7% of the population in the 2001 census – so teachers, governors and parents often say, 'There's no racism here'. What they mean is, 'We have so few non-white children at school that we get few racist incidents.' But under the surface may be prejudiced attitudes that grow unchallenged.

Research suggests that racism is particularly strong in Cumbria. According to the *Cumbrian Attitudes Survey,* produced by Cumbria County Council and Cumbria Constabulary in 2005, almost three quarters of its population admit to being prejudiced against at least one minority group, and 35% of those express prejudices towards three or more groups. Both these figures are higher than the national average (64% and 16%) and expose the assumption, often expressed in predominantly white communities, that 'there's no problem here'. Prejudice is particularly marked in relation to refugees and asylum seekers and to Gypsies and Travellers.

At my previous school, a church school in Cumbria, we had a memorial assembly a year after 9/11. A parent led the assembly and, unbelievably, made this statement: 'Anyone who isn't white, we can't trust them'. I was shocked and, even worse, neither the headteacher nor any other staff mentioned it or seemed surprised. All the children heard this and it was not challenged. I left soon after.
Cumbrian primary school teacher speaking in March 2005

To avoid the dangers of institutional racism, as well as challenge prejudice and stereotypes held by pupils, schools must also address the views held by the adults, including all school staff.

Research by Chris Wilkins at Reading University found that one in ten trainee teachers on post-graduate teacher training courses hold racist views. It can't be assumed that support for the racist views of extreme right wing parties doesn't come from some teachers, governors, lunchtime supervisors or school site managers.

In many predominantly white communities it is assumed that racism is 'treating people differently because of

their skin colour' and there can be denial that other types of racism, such as simplistic or patronising attitudes, are also damaging. The significance of cultural and ethnic diversity can be underplayed, while the acceptance of a one-size-fits-all approach can discourage ethnic minority pupils from appreciating and expressing important aspects of their identity and culture. So the challenge is not just for teachers to explore attitudes in the classroom, but also for them to look at the attitudes that exist in the staffroom and in the whole school community.

How do we know what attitudes our teachers, governors, and support staff hold and how these may be transmitted to pupils?

Teachers in mainly white schools are more comfortable looking outwards to other countries for contrasting localities and opportunities to incorporate multicultural education, rather than drawing on the diversity and confronting the prejudice towards other cultures within their own communities. This is reflected in the numbers of international school links and culture week projects carried out by schools. Teachers can find

CARLISLE BEST OF BRITISH, SAYS BNP MAN

From an article in *The News and Star*, Cumbria 15/09/2003

CARLISLE has been cited as the last bastion of traditional British identity by one of the leading lights of the far-right British National Party. Wigton-based Martin Wingfield, who edits the BNP's newspaper, *Voice of Freedom*, compared virtually all-white Carlisle with other multicultural British cities in a speech to the party's recent Red White and Blue festival. His comments have been branded as 'objectionable' by a senior Labour politician.

Mr Wingfield described a Saturday shopping trip to Carlisle when he came across morris dancers, a brass band and a Christian convention. He said: 'There was something else special about this Saturday afternoon scene and that was the people who were milling around. 'They were English, Scottish, Irish, Ulster and Welsh. All true Brits stretching back generations. I can assure you that there was no other British city like Carlisle that afternoon. Yet do you think our opponents would have been celebrating that diversity? Would they have been holding up Carlisle as a fine example of the difference that enriches our culture? No, unfortunately not. To them, traditional Britishness is something that must be stamped out. They would want Carlisle to have steel bands and melas and an influx of ten to twenty thousand newcomers from Africa, Asia and Eastern Europe, just to bring it in line with other British cities. The 'celebrating diversity' they talk about is the destruction of the British identity.'

---

it difficult to explore the hard issues of diversity and prejudice closer to home. Education for equality in mainly white schools is not just about other places, cultures and ethnicities. It needs to reflect diversity within the local and regional communities because diversity is about much more than ethnicity, and predominantly white communities are diverse in many other ways.

The attitude that says 'go back to where you came from' is levelled at incomers of many kinds. People in some areas of Cumbria experience a form of tribalism. At its extreme, you are one of the 'out group' if you don't belong to the few original local families or have a particular surname. Moving from one village to a neighbouring one, or from one estate to another, can turn you into an outsider. Local children do not choose to hold these attitudes, they inherit them.

Teachers are not immune from this tribalism. For example, during an activity at a race equality training course at a

---

Teachers can empower pupils by exploring with them the usual stages in the development of prejudice

We are not born with prejudice, we learn it. Prejudice means 'pre-judging':

■ Judging, assuming or expressing an opinion before having all the correct information

■ Judging a person or a group of people simply because they act or appear different from us

It is usual to move through the following stages when we develop prejudicial behaviour:

1. That person is different from me and therefore is inferior to me

2. That person is no good

3. That person is my enemy

4. That person is a threat to my safety and security, and to my family or group

5. I must defend myself against my enemy, and my group against 'them'

6. I feel inner conflict and I project my conflict onto my enemy

7. Sooner or later we are going to fight

Prejudice can end when we observe these stages, in the making, in our own mind. Once we observe it we can stop it.

Perceptions of Cumbria:

Cumbria is so attractive – I love the sheep and the farms in the Lake District National Park.

I can't afford to run my farm. The global economy is threatening farming traditions because the per-head return on traditional breeds of sheep barely allows farmers to break even on their flocks.

I'm drawn to the Lake District because of the quiet beauty of the fells.

Visitors are causing the breakup of village communities, because most young people born within the Lake District National Park cannot afford to buy a home here. So they leave.

We love sailing and being at one with nature.

Where I live has a population of 6000, and 1 million visitors each year come to my village and take a cruise on the lake. This influx is devastating the sense of cohesion and community in my neighbourhood.

It's so quiet and clean and safe here. I don't notice the nuclear power station...

Cumbria covers an area larger than Lancashire, Merseyside, Greater Manchester and Cheshire combined. Most of the population lives outside the boundaries of the National Park, many in areas suffering economic depression hand-in-hand with disenchanted youth, drug abuse, poverty and hardship.

I'd love to buy that old barn and do it up and live in a rural idyll.

The gap between wages and house prices within the National Park is now so great that in one village 70% of houses are second homes. People born locally are unlikely to stay.

I'd love to work here, not just holiday here.

The myriad of seasonal tourism jobs are filled by high numbers of temporary migrant workers, many from Eastern Europe.

school in Workington in 2004, some teachers expressed hostility towards people from the neighbouring town of Whitehaven. The insult used was 'jam eater', referring to the habit of having only jam on your sandwiches because of extreme poverty. Several staff became red in the face and distressed at being called this name by someone who came from the other town and replied: 'No, it's not us, it's you!' This incident stems from rivalry between the mining communities, played out on the sports field and continued today.

Exploring attitudes to diversity within their community is a challenge for teachers, so exploring differing perceptions of Cumbria is an interesting place to start.

When they think of Cumbria, many people think of sheep and lakes, a beautiful environment, farming and rural communities who are lucky to live there. This is a stereotyped view, far from the whole truth. Ordering our understanding of the world in stereotypes provides a framework for information that needs to be questioned and evaluated. Our stereotypes are fuelled by our expectations, so what we expect to find is generally what we do find. While each view of Cumbria is valid, none is complete. In Cumbria, as everywhere else, diversity is the norm.

Some secondary teachers in Cumbria face the challenge of how, through the curriculum, to address the fact that local adults hand out extreme right wing and blatantly racist material to pupils near the school gates. So what are primary teachers in Cumbria doing to prepare their pupils to develop the judgement and moral courage to stand against such prejudice when they meet it? This book gives a sample of the good practice that is taking place in the county.

Through this book we offer a range of examples that are relevant to other predominantly white areas of the UK, to help staff and pupils in three important ways:

■ tackling their preconceptions and seeing people for who they are, not as a stereotype

■ questioning what they *think* they know about others

■ learning the skills that enable them to see life from another's perspective

Section 1 features a range of activities that reveal some of the attitudes held in schools where, at first glance, it might seem 'there is no problem here'. By exploring, unpacking and reflecting on the attitudes held towards others, teachers and pupils can take a first step towards recognising, acknowledging and changing the damaging prejudiced and racist attitudes that exist – in Cumbria and beyond.

■ 1.1: I live here and I think ... perceptions of a locality

This activity was devised to help pupils reflect on their perceptions of places, and was part of a school linking project involving two Cumbrian schools in contrasting locations (see section 1.2). This part of the project took place in a primary school in a socially deprived neighbourhood with 120 pupils on role.

Large sheets of paper were prepared with three columns. Locations were chosen from the streets where pupils in the class live, and one of the chosen street names was written at the top of each sheet. The sheets were displayed so the class could complete this task over several weeks.

This relatively long time-scale was important. The school has a high proportion of pupils facing serious social and personal disadvantage and some have special educational needs. It

ensured that all the pupils were able to engage fully with the activity and were comfortable about expressing their honest opinions.

Outcomes

During this activity the pupils talked about their home lives and experiences, including some of the prejudices they knew were held against the streets they live in. When discussing one of the streets near the school, a pupil said, 'They say they've heard it is full of burnt out cars, but I like it, my Nan lives there'.

Through this activity the pupils experienced how it feels to hear a negative or stereotypical view expressed about the place that for them is home. It was a useful learning experience, making real the fact that whatever people have heard about a place is often all that they know, and that hearing only one view isn't enough.

Woodsghyll Drive		
I live here and I think....	I've been here and I think.....	I've heard....
It's not busy. It is close to the school but you wouldn't like to live here because it is busy and dangerous.	• Too close to school but a nice street. • We don't like some people here. • It's boring because there is nothing to do. • A lot of my friends live here.	• There are a lot of smashed windows. • It's boring and noisy. • It is dangerous because of the cars and you can get run over.

Comments by pupils about a street in their neighbourhood.

Follow-up and adaptations

This activity can be used in a range of contexts. For example, CDEC used it as part of teacher in-service training that focused on the importance of recognising prevailing perceptions. Participants were asked where they live and from these places five villages or towns were chosen. The names were written at the top of the prepared sheets. Participants circulated around the room writing honest comments about each place in the relevant column on each sheet. Enough time was allowed for everyone to write on every sheet. A whole-group feedback began with one person who lives in the place reading out the comments, one sheet at a time, and the group reflecting on them.

The statements teachers wrote reflected not just their knowledge about places but also much hearsay. Taken together, these reflected the range of perceptions and stereotypes about Cumbrian localities among Cumbrian residents. The difference between the statements commonly made by people who live in a place and those who have only visited or heard about it provoked a great deal of questioning dialogue. Understanding this range of perceptions about places close to home that we know well gives us an indication of the preconceptions about places and people we have heard about only in the media or visited on holiday. The teachers agreed that this was a useful starting point not only for themselves but also for their pupils, and many teachers subsequently used it in the classroom.

This activity can also be used to consider places in other countries. It provides an assessment of existing attitudes before pupils learn about another locality or work on an international school link. It can be adapted to consider perceptions of other people by selecting relevant groups in the local context (e.g. Gypsies and Travellers). Once pupils are able to identify and challenge their perceptions of other people within their own community, they can expand this skill to consider diversity in the wider world.

■ 1.2: Perceptions of a contrasting locality within a region

This activity was part of a school linking project between two contrasting schools: one with 120 pupils in a socially deprived urban area, and the other with 60 pupils in a rural village. The link was instigated by the National Trust as part of its education programme in Cumbria and was further supported by CDEC. The link aimed to bring together schools from different backgrounds to work on shared arts projects. Pupils in Years 3, 4, 5 and 6 were involved.

A significant feature of this project was the difference in the social context and culture of the two schools. This made partnership working a challenge and also brought a range of opportunities for widening pupils' horizons. In the urban school, only five pupils from a class of 24 had been on a train before, and few had travelled out of their local surroundings. In the rural school, few pupils had walked through town streets unaccompanied by relatives.

Teachers' comments about one group of people who live in the neighbourhood.

I am an... offcomer and I think	I know an... offcomer and I think	I've heard
We can't help where our parents choose to bring us up. Am I an offcomer when I move from Windermere to Ambleside? I have to go more than half-way to create new friendships. I always will be – I've only lived here 25 yrs!	We are all just people who live somewhere. Some can be a bit 'busy-body' and this doesn't help the reputation.	Cumbrian communities don't like new people, off-comers. They sometimes complain about the locals and that annoys me.

I am a... farmer and I think	I know a... farmer and I think	I've heard
It's my heritage and an important part of my identity, even though I didn't take over the farm but my brother did.	They can be very stubborn and difficult. They can be friendly and helpful, the opposite to what you would think. Some are quite rich and pretend not to be. They all seem to work hard.	They got used to huge subsidies in the 80s and still expect it. They have a hard time with sheep farming, not much return for hours of work. They are wealthy but some aren't. They have a strong community.

Session 1: Pupils in each school spent an afternoon walking around their own locality to explore the environment and undertake a local audit. They agreed on twelve significant aspects of their local environment that were important to them and recorded these with cameras and tape recorders.

Session 2: Pupils in each school considered their existing perceptions about the other school's environment. At the urban school they were asked to write down 'words that come to mind when you think of a rural school'. They responded with words like 'friendly, peaceful, no bad behaviour, different language and boring'. Likewise pupils at the rural school were asked to write down 'words that come to mind when you think of an urban school'. Their responses included words like 'skyscrapers, good shopping, drunks at night, dangerous and queues'.

Pupils then explored the twelve significant aspects in the pictures and sound recordings sent to them by their link school. They were given time to study these to get a better idea of what the environment of the other school was really like, and to review and reconsider their initial perceptions. This enabled them to list similarities and differences between their own school environment and that of their partner school.

Outcomes

This project continued with a joint art activity described in section 4.7. Following the art project, the urban school returned to the twelve significant aspects they had identified in their own neighbourhood during the initial audit. Some of these had been chosen because they were seen as special and important, others because they were a problem and the pupils wanted them to change. For example the riverside was identified as a place where pupils meet their friends and have fun, but it was also seen as dirty and the pupils felt that some people do not look after it. This contrasted with their perception of the river in a rural location which they said would be clean and well looked after.

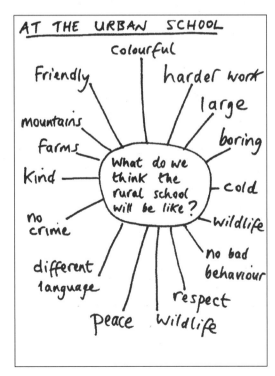

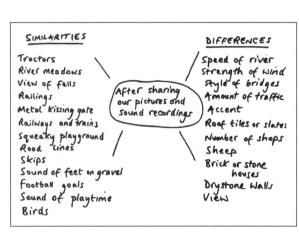

Similarities and differences identified by pupils, after hearing about each other's neighbourhoods.

ZOE'S STORY

I drew the fish because some times I go swimming in the river and see the fishes. I think the river isn't clean because there are fields near the river and there is soil in the river and all the waste goes in. I wish the council would clean the river so we won't get ill and more people will swim in the river.

The pupils used their reflections on the special features of their environment to write stories about places that were significant in their lives, both positively and negatively. These stories were put together in a book and used to stimulate philosophical enquiry. This allowed further exploration of the perceptions of a contrasting locality within the region and promoted awareness of different environments.

■ 1.3: Perceptions of Britain – a diverse society

This unit for Year 4 pupils took place in a primary school with over 400 pupils. It ran for one session per week over five weeks in two parallel classes. It was adapted by the class teacher from Unit 5 *Living in a Diverse World* in the QCA/DfES *Scheme of Work for Citizenship*.

Session 1 – aimed to help pupils understand that the way someone looks or dresses is not an indication of where they live

Pupils were shown a selection of sixteen photographs of children from a range of different cultures and ethnicities and asked to write down where they thought each of the children was from, and why. They were asked to write down whether they could tell anything about the children by the way they were dressed.

The teacher was surprised and disappointed to hear the many stereotypical responses showing that the pupils generally believed that:

■ all the white children were from Britain

■ the black child must be poor and come from Africa

■ the parents of the Chinese child must be receptionists (they had seen Chinese hotel workers whilst on holiday)

■ the ginger-haired child must be Scottish

Discussion followed to help pupils consider whether we can really tell where a person is from just by the way they look. Pupils questioned the idea of national dress: whether it is typical in any country, what British national dress might look like and why agreeing on one isn't easy. As a result, pupils began to accept that appearance or dress do not automatically indicate the country a person is from, and that the UK is home to a wide variety of cultures and ethnicities.

Session 2 – aimed to help pupils understand that a range of elements contribute to make up a person's identity

Pupils were asked to draw a picture showing what they think a British person looks like. This served as a baseline indication of the pupils' understanding of multicultural Britain. Most of their pictures showed a white British person.

The teacher led a circle time activity at which:

■ Pupils found something similar between themselves and another person in the circle

■ Pupils found something different between themselves and another person in the circle

■ Differences were discussed, highlighting how these make us unique and give us our individual identities

■ Pupils discussed, with a partner, the needs all humans have in common, such as water, food and shelter. They listed the differences between people, for example their languages, hobbies and jobs

■ The discussion was widened to include the national context: 'If you went to London, what would be the same and what would be different?'

> Some pupils said: 'anyone who isn't white is a tourist'.

> So the teacher challenged their ideas to help them realise their mistaken perceptions.

■ Each pupil thought of something special about themselves, shared it with their partner who reported back to the circle

> What is special about me is that I am kind and if anybody is hurt I will look after them

> My knees click

> I have nice friends and family

■ The session ended with a circle time game of 'silent statements' where, for example, the teacher said, 'Change places if you have felt hurt by being left out'

Session 3 aimed to help pupils form their own opinions that might contradict a stereotype

The sixteen photos used in the first session were again displayed around the room, along with fifteen job titles. The pupils worked in groups to discuss which of the children in the photos they thought would have each job when they grew up. As a class they shared their responses and discussed their reasoning. There was a class vote and the results were recorded.

There was strong agreement by pupils, even though there was a choice of sixteen photos and fifteen job titles. Ethnicity and gender both played a role in the choices and the reasons given. One child was voted most likely to become a police officer 'because he looks fierce'; another to be Prime Minister 'because of the way he is dressed'; another to be a nurse 'because she looks caring'; another to be a businessman 'because he looks like he has had a good education'. The boy most widely believed to be British was considered likely to become a window cleaner 'because he doesn't look like he's capable of much'. Until the teacher pointed it out, none of the pupils volunteered the view that any of the children might have any of the jobs when they grew up.

Session 4 aimed to help pupils learn that it is wrong to tease someone because they are different

The class was shown a different selection of photos depicting people of different ages, genders, backgrounds, appearance and dress. Pupils were asked to:

■ sort the pictures according to their own criteria

■ give reasons why they put some people into one group and not another

■ find similarities and differences between themselves and the people in the photos

■ consider which group they might fit into

A discussion followed, focusing on some of the reasons why some people might be teased if they look different, and whether this is acceptable. This led to a discussion about prejudice and racial intolerance.

Session 5 aimed to help pupils understand that some people are threatened by difference

The class was shown the original set of photos and asked to discuss their responses to the following questions:

■ Who are you most like?

■ Who looks like the most honest person and the most dishonest?

- Who would you most like to be friends with or not be friends with?

- Who would you trust with a secret?

- Who will get the best job when they are older?

- Who would you feel threatened by?

Pupils were challenged to give reasons for their answers, and to say why they did not see the children in the photos as having an equal weighting. After this discussion, pupils again drew a picture of their idea of what a British person might look like. Many pupils included elements of diversity in these second drawings,

and when asked whether they thought all white people are British (and all British people are white), everyone agreed that the answer is no.

Outcomes and reflections

The pupils enjoyed this unit and were pleased when they saw the photographs again. The teacher evaluated it as successful but also as an ongoing process, because not all the pupils had understood the issues in any depth. She decided to expand the unit and use it in future years.

When reflecting on their learning, pupils made these comments

Pupil's drawing of a British person with the label: 'All the people on Earth are different'.

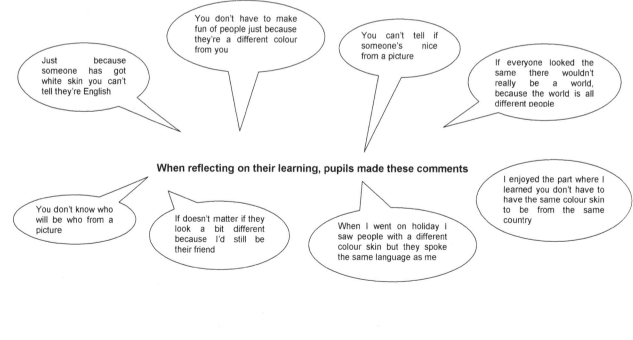

When reflecting on their learning, pupils made these comments

Just because someone has got white skin you can't tell they're English

You don't have to make fun of people just because they're a different colour from you

You can't tell if someone's nice from a picture

If everyone looked the same there wouldn't really be a world, because the world is all different people

You don't know who will be who from a picture

If doesn't matter if they look a bit different because I'd still be their friend

When I went on holiday I saw people with a different colour skin but they spoke the same language as me

I enjoyed the part where I learned you don't have to have the same colour skin to be from the same country

■ 1.4: All about me ... exploring my own identity

This project was part of a series of weekly philosophical enquiry sessions introducing moral dilemmas to a Year 4 class. It was led by CDEC over the course of a school term in a primary school with over 200 pupils. Philosophy for Children (P4C) was being introduced across the whole school as a way of developing skilful thinking.

Session 1

Pupils were asked to consider their own identity. They were given eleven statements and asked to choose any three that would be important if they were to describe themselves to another person.

After choosing their statements individually, whole-class feedback showed that the most popular choice was 'what I look like'.

In order to challenge the view that it is easy to know someone simply from their appearance, the pupils were shown a picture taken from *Values for Thinking* by Robert Fisher (Nash Pollock Publishing) which shows a uniformed policeman apparently chasing a black man. The pupils were asked to say what they thought was happening and they all agreed that this showed a policeman chasing a thief. When told that the black man was also a policeman but in plain clothes, they were surprised. They realised that they had jumped to

inappropriate conclusions based on mere appearance.

The session ended by pupils considering:

Would you rather be ... ?

■ A peasant woman from Guatemala or a Nobel Prize winner

■ A single mother of three children or a well-paid surgeon

■ A homeless man living in Manchester or a university graduate

■ A disabled wheelchair user or a famous marathon winner

After some discussion about the choices and the pupils' ideas, it was explained that each pair of statements referred to the same person. This led to surprise and further dialogue about the different ways people can be described.

Session 2

Pupils discussed information on Socrates, questioning and philosophy. An apple was shown and questions were asked about it such as: 'What is an apple? What are the parts that make up an apple?' The apple was peeled and the children were asked: 'Is it still an apple?' They all agreed that it was. The apple was cut into quarters and the core taken out and the children were asked: 'Is it still an apple? What can we take away and there still be an apple?' There was no consensus this time – the pupils weren't sure!

- What I do in my spare time
- Who I play with
- The clothes I wear
- Bad things I have done
- Where my parents come from
- The stories I like
- What I look like
- My beliefs and values
- My ideas about the world
- Good things I have done
- Where I live

After discussing the apple, the children were asked: 'What is a human being? What are the parts that make up a person?' Pupils agreed about this and named various body parts. When they were asked 'What can we take away and there still be the same person?' there was no agreement.

Pupils were referred back to the eleven statements of identity used in the previous session and asked: 'If we changed each of these in ourselves, would we be the same person?'

Outcomes

Pupils reflected on their experiences in using philosophy to explore ideas about themselves and others. They said:

> I liked the games we played and that if we disagreed with somebody we weren't being nasty but we just discussed it
>
> We listened to each other
>
> We thought about what other people said
>
> I learned how much we can read into things
>
> I liked when we split the apple and asked if it was still an apple
>
> Philosophy helps me think deeper into things

■ 1.5: I am a Cumbrian and who are you?

This project was led by CDEC, with Years 4 and 5, in a primary school with over 200 pupils in a small market town. The aim was to explore and consider the perceptions that pupils held about the different people who live in Cumbria.

Introductory activity

Pupils were asked to say which words came to mind when thinking of Cumbria and the people who live there. The responses from Year 5 pupils included: 'me; farms; hills; friendly; countryside; kind; helpful; fit and sport; cool; proper Cumbrians have a funny accent; sheep'. Responses from Year 4 pupils included: 'I only know my cousin; kind people; no accent; small; white skin'.

With whom do I identify?

The pupils were shown photographs of a diverse range of people from across Cumbria, including: Travellers; farmers; crowded and flooded streets in Carlisle; windsurfing off Walney Island; Buddhist monks at Conishead Priory; black people on the streets of Carlisle; the mosque in Carlisle; and a landfill site. Pupils were asked to look at each photo and indicate those they thought were taken in Cumbria with a white sticker, and those that they thought were taken outside Cumbria with a red sticker.

Enough time was allowed for all the pupils to complete the task. The ideas behind their choices were discussed as a whole class, using prompting questions such as: 'Why did everyone think this picture was not in Cumbria?, or 'Why do you think there was so much disagreement over whether this picture is from Cumbria?'. A range of views held by the pupils were considered and challenged. They were very surprised that all the pictures were in fact taken in Cumbria.

Perceptions that Cumbria is a quiet, clean place were expressed with comments such as:

> It's too messy for Cumbria
>
> It's too rough looking and there's no countryside
>
> I can see villages so it must be Cumbria
>
> That sort of thing happens normally in cities

Perceptions that religious and ethnic diversity doesn't belong in Cumbria were expressed with comments such as:

> I don't think we have temples in Cumbria
>
> There are too many black people for it to be Cumbria
>
> You wouldn't find people here who pray like that

Some interesting misconceptions of geography were expressed with comments such as:

- There's no ports, big ships or areas like that in Cumbria
- There's no sea on the outside of Cumbria
- It doesn't rain that much in Cumbria
- It looks like an old fashioned horse-riding place

Who am I?

The project moved onto misconceptions about people and how easy it is to fall into the trap of stereotyping when we only have a little information about someone. A pair of statements was shown and the whole class were asked to give their ideas about what kind of person the statements described. Other statements were discussed in the same way, one pair at a time.

'It's me!'. Pupils were surprised to find the statements were all true about one person.

Pupils suggested a range of ideas about the person they thought each pair of statements might describe. They expressed surprise and intrigue when shown a photo of the session leader and told that all the statements were about this one person rather than describing lots of different people.

- I have arthritis
- I can't see very well

- I came second in a fell race
- I climbed all the Lake District mountains before the age of 15

- I live on a council-built housing estate
- My house is very noisy

- I have written three books
- I have been to over one hundred classical music concerts

- I think sheep are very interesting, especially Herdwicks
- I helped give birth to lambs

- I used to live in India
- I grew up in a city

- My best friend lives in America
- I used to own a guest house in the Lake District

Discussion followed about specific facts and why the pupils thought some statements couldn't apply to the same person. For example, living on a council-built housing estate and having owned a guesthouse were considered incompatible because one person would be poor and the other rich. There was agreement that we need a lot of information about someone before we can really know what kind of person they are, and that our first judgements can be wrong. The activity powerfully conveyed this message because the children were curious about their teacher and because the learning happened through making wrong judgements.

Pupils were asked to reflect on these key questions:

■ If we only know one thing about someone, how much do we know them?

■ When we know what someone looks like, do we make judgements about their personality?

■ Are Cumbrians all the same?

■ What is a person from your town like?

Unique Faces of Britain

Britain – we all make it unique

As a plenary, pupils were shown the poster entitled *Britain – We all make it Unique* produced by the Commission for Racial Equality. The pupils were asked to describe what they saw and their responses were: 'all different'; 'men, women and children'; 'all live in Britain'; 'people from all round the world'; 'all look different'; 'different religions'; 'might have different accents'; 'from different countries but live in Britain'. One Year 4 pupil expressed the views of many by asking, 'They don't all live in Britain do they?'

Outcomes

Pupils looked back at the statements about Cumbria they made at the beginning of the session to consider whether they had changed their minds. When asked what they had learned through this activity, they gave a range of responses. One child wanted to talk after the session and had the following exchange with the session leader:

> Pupil: '*There's something that I've learned … it means now I know why my Dad says he hates black people*'
>
> Leader: '*Can you tell me more about what you mean by that?*'
>
> Pupil: '*He said all the, what is it, Muslims are bad. He says they bombed people.*'

> Leader: '*So what do you think about these things that he says?*'
>
> Pupil: '*Well you can't say that, it doesn't mean they are all the same, I think he is wrong*'

This pupil came from a family with strong views. Her father had complained about her taking part in a topic on Buddhism the previous term, and at a parents' evening had proudly told the class teacher, 'I am a racist'. It is important to help pupils develop thinking skills so they can make informed judgments for themselves, and avoid inheriting stereotypical views by default.

The class teacher observing this session said, 'It was really powerful. It provoked some fascinating responses from the children which highlighted misconceptions even in the brightest and most able'.

Follow-up

The Year 4 class teacher led a follow-up activity. A set of pictures was shown on the interactive whiteboard, including a black youth, an elderly white woman, various smiling faces, and people with other facial expressions. The pupils were asked to say where they thought each person in the pictures might come from, and they tended to say that those with a black face come from Africa, or that black people who do live in Cumbria couldn't have been born there. The pupils then discussed whether it was possible to tell what religion each person might belong to, just from seeing their picture.

Finally the pupils were asked which of the people in the pictures might have recently broken the law. At first they talked about ways in which the black youth might have broken the law, but with further discussion and suggestion from the teacher, realised that it could have been anyone, including possibly the old lady!

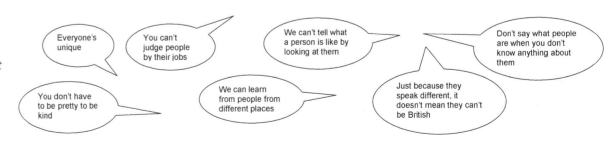

Everyone's unique

You can't judge people by their jobs

We can't tell what a person is like by looking at them

Don't say what people are when you don't know anything about them

You don't have to be pretty to be kind

We can learn from people from different places

Just because they speak different, it doesn't mean they can't be British

■ 1.6: Finding out about me

This was a Reception class topic at a primary school with 200 pupils, where a few pupils have family origins in Senegal, Hong Kong and the USA, a small number wear a hearing aid, and some have statements of special needs including children on the autistic spectrum.

The school aims to present an inclusive ethos, where everyone understands that difference is not something to be ashamed of, and where everyone is treated equally. For instance a Year 6 pupil with Asperger's syndrome was given class time to talk about his condition, about the ways in which it makes him different from the others, and how it affects his learning and communication skills. This helped the other pupils and staff understand him better, and he gained greater acceptance for his sometimes disruptive behaviour.

The school has established a link with a primary school in Bradford where 70% of the pupils have South Asian heritage and are mainly Muslims with some Hindus. Year 6 pupils have exchanged letters, visited and made curriculum links. The school is also planning to establish a link with a school in another country, and is considering how the Reception class might be involved.

A patchwork to represent each pupil

Early in their first term in Reception class, pupils took home a square of cloth to decorate in a personal way using photos, magazine pictures, words and patterns. They were asked to feature things such as their favourite activities or toys. The class looked at and discussed each pupil's square as they were returned, and talked about the things they have in common with others in the class, particularly the interesting things they didn't know about their classmates.

All the squares were sewn together by a parent, and the resulting patchwork was used throughout the year as a focus for talking about themselves and each other. For example pupils identified things that are similar to their own likes and interests, and they discussed all the ways in which they are different. This was done with an underlying emphasis on each person being equally valued despite these differences. The class teacher used this patchwork as a starting point for further stories, activities and topics, in particular those with a focus on differences and similarities.

A pupil had joined the Reception class after moving to Cumbria from the USA, and she was feeling isolated and homesick. This project helped her to identify other pupils in the class who have similar interests and she was able to find friends and settle into the group.

Pupils each made a square for the quilt

Feelings Tree

The class teacher made a *Feelings Tree* with a range of photos of faces hanging on the branches, and some loose leaves in red and green paper. Each morning the pupils knew to choose a leaf, either a red one to represent feeling unhappy, or a green one to represent feeling happy. They hung their leaf next to the face on the tree that best reflected their feelings that day. The faces showed various emotions: happy, sad, angry and worried, as expressed by children and adults from a range of ethnic backgrounds. This showed the pupils that all kinds of people experience different emotions, no matter what they look like.

This daily activity enabled the class teacher to identify pupils who came to school feeling upset, sad or angry, so she could give support where it was most needed. It was very important in tackling pupils' problems before their emotions led to behaviours that disrupted the rest of the class.

Pupils made clay faces of themselves

Clay faces

The teacher took a large photograph of each pupil in her class. These were displayed alongside some of the faces from the *Feelings Tree*, which included the green-faced Princess Fiona from the cartoon Shrek. Pupils were given time to look closely at the pictures so that they could consider and compare their features.

The pupils commented on differences and similarities between themselves and others in the class, especially focusing on skin colour. None of the pupils liked the look of the green-faced person, and in fact they barely recognised it as a person. The class concluded that it was okay for a person to be shades of brown, pink and black, but not green. With further questioning the pupils agreed that Princess Fiona was not a horrible person, but that they thought she looked horrible.

After comparing the various skin colours, each pupil mixed a paint colour close to their own skin tone and made and painted a clay face to resemble themselves.

Outcomes

Once pupils began to find out about themselves they began to realise that people are all different, not just in skin colour but in many ways. In this project pupils learned that emotions, not just physical appearance, are part of what makes up a person. Once young children learn to talk about emotions by identifying their feelings, they can start learning how to manage these feelings. In this project pupils learned that other people experience the same intensity of feelings, and that one person's actions can affect other people. They learned that it is normal to be angry sometimes, or not to like someone, and talking about feelings is appropriate whereas hitting out is not. They began to talk about the reasons for their feelings, giving good explanations and respecting the reasons and feelings of others.

■ 1.7: Baseline assessment

The setting for this project was an infant school with over 200 pupils. The majority of pupils are of white British origin with a few from other ethnic groups, some with English as an additional language, and some with dual language heritage. The sessions were led by an advisory teacher from Cumbria Education Service.

The staff had introduced their pupils to a range of multicultural activities, including the hosting of a Japanese intern who worked with pupils. Staff worked on global issues, took part in an INSET day at the Bradford Interfaith Centre and attended a variety of courses on multicultural and antiracist issues. So they were genuinely surprised when an Ofsted inspection report noted that there was insufficient evidence of multicultural education in the school.

Motivated by this and by the need to implement their Race Equality Policy, a range of activities were planned with the advisory teacher for a mixed Year 1 and 2 class. Regular Philosophy for Children sessions (see sections 4.3 and 4.4) also followed throughout the year.

Pupils were asked to look closely at some photos of children who might or might not live in this country, taken from the *Alphabet Photo Frieze of Children Around the World* (NES Arnold, £9.99). When shown the picture of Tola the first response was 'She's got darker skin so she lives in Africa or a hot country'. This openness was unusual as often the colour of skin is not mentioned by pupils because they have learned, wrongly, that it is rude. The comment also reflected a commonly-held view among children in rural areas that black people must live in Africa and not the UK.

With the 26 photos spread around the classroom, pupils in mixed Year 1/Year 2 pairs were asked to look at each photo and decide: 'Which children could have come from a country other than this one?' They were given red stickers to put on the photos of children who they thought do live in this country and green stickers to put on those who don't. They had to agree their choices in their pairs.

This activity led to some pupils discussing with their partners what was meant by 'this country'. One child thought Ewen was from Wales and wasn't sure whether Wales is part of 'this country'. Do we mean England, Great Britain or the United Kingdom? The pictures stimulated much discussion, influenced by the pupils' own experiences of travel and TV.

At first a few pupils laughed at some of the names (for example Dozzie), but one pupil quickly responded that names are not something to laugh at, a view that was supported by others in the class.

Another pupil noticed that one of the names was the same as that of a boy in the class, but they couldn't decide if the picture was of a boy or a girl. This confusion led to discussion about whether it is possible to know things about people just by looking at them or just by knowing their name. The pupils' reaction to unfamiliar names was noted for follow-up.

Once all the stickers had been placed, the class discussed why certain choices had been made. Photos with just red stickers received comments such as 'They have the same colour skin as ours' and 'All the people in India have black hair'. Photos with green stickers received comments such as: 'They have browner skin and their eyes are different' and 'I knew that red is a lucky colour in China'. Statements were challenged and sometimes the pupils questioned each other's opinions, for example: 'Some have the same colour skin as us but could live in Wales or America'.

Discussion ensued about the six pictures that had received both red and green dots. Initially, few pupils supported the idea that children in the photos could live anywhere in the world. They named a pupil in the class who had been born in Australia and had the same colour skin as pupils born locally. One pupil suggested that 'those with brown skins could have moved here' and 'You can have a brown skin and live in a cold country like Canada'. Another said 'There are some people with darker skins who live here'.

At this point it dawned on the pupils that one of their classmates had dark skin. They knew he had moved from Pakistan to live locally. Most of the pupils said that people with 'brown skins' would have come from hot countries so the teacher had to reinforce the point that they could also be born here.

Reference was made to the photo that bore the same name as a pupil in the class. Pupils agreed that having the same name didn't mean they came from the same place, and one pupil summed up the discussion by saying, 'We can share things – like names. We can have things in common, but we aren't the same'.

One girl asked if people could ever be the same, and because there were twins in

Pupils with their chosen pictures.

the class the teacher encouraged pupils to question them about their likes and dislikes. The twins' answers illustrated that they were each unique individuals even though they looked similar.

The discussion focused on the different languages that the pupils or their parents, grandparents or other relatives could speak. Two pupils with English as an additional language (one Pakistani and one Swedish) were proud of their linguistic abilities and their classmates were interested that these pupils could speak more than one language. This led to the pupils agreeing on the importance of focusing on and celebrating what they shared, not just focusing on their differences.

The pupils were shown the 26 photos again and asked to choose one child with whom they felt they shared something. The reasons they gave were:

We share the same hairstyle and colour of eyes
We share the same colour of skin and the same pattern of T-shirt
We share freckles and the same size ears
We share similar long hair
I think he is from Pakistan like me
We share the same shape of mouth – our smile

Future activities

This activity was followed by an afternoon session which is described in section 4.4. It was the beginning of a longer-term programme of antiracist and global awareness activities that the school is still developing.

Outcomes

Activities similar to this have been carried out by CDEC and by advisory teachers with many schools in Cumbria, often in the context of setting up a link with a partner school overseas. The term 'baseline assessment' reflects the long-term aims of this type of session. It is not intended as a stand-alone activity because pupils' and teacher's knowledge and perceptions should be revisited and reviewed as part of an ongoing process.

CDEC, in partnership with Global Link and Lancashire Global Education Centre, has produced the *Lancashire Cumbria Photopack*. It includes pictures representing a range of topics and situations relevant to the different people who live in Cumbria and Lancashire, and this has been useful in baseline assessment sessions.

Baseline assessment activities can help teachers to see and hear the preconceptions held by their pupils. This is vital if they are to plan their longer-term programmes to challenge prejudices and avoid these being reinforced. In the context of school linking, discussed in section 4.6, it enables the teachers and pupils to have an open and honest dialogue about their views about other people and places, before a dialogue with real people in those places begins.

Assumptions about others

There are some assumptions made by pupils from Cumbria as part of a school linking project carried out by CDEC and funded by the Department for International Development (DfID).

Pupils looked at and categorised photographs from the wider world as a stimulus for dialogue. These are some of the things they said:

There are no black people in my country

They have no money to buy shoes there

People aren't as poor here as in Africa

They don't need trainers as much as I do

The problems are because there are too many people living there

They can't have computers because they don't have electricity

People who are poor have no friends

Poor countries are hot, and rich countries are cold

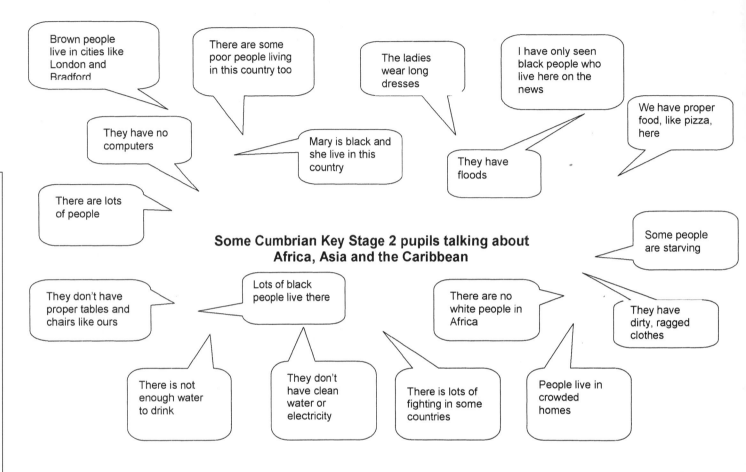

Some Cumbrian Key Stage 2 pupils talking about Africa, Asia and the Caribbean

How do we embed equality in whole-school practice?

For multicultural and antiracist education to have lasting impact in mainly white schools it is vital that it is not delivered as a series of stand-alone activities. It needs to be part of a whole-school ethos driven by clear principles and promoted throughout the wider school community.

The motivation for a whole-school approach often comes from the headteacher's drive and enthusiasm, either in response to external events or as a result of one or two pivotal activities taking place within the school. It is important that the core values are shared and that an antiracist ethos is embraced by all staff, including recently qualified teachers and non-teaching staff. Ensuring that all staff and governors have ownership of the antiracist agenda can be more difficult than educating pupils about antiracism.

Achieving a whole-school approach to antiracism depends on the senior staff and governors, taking the issues seriously over a sustained period. Race equality is a long-term goal that can't be achieved quickly. The process remains tokenistic if teachers think they have finished once an activity is complete.

Activities need to be embedded in a long-term programme.

False starts can be made

■ if activities are add-on (such as *Divali Day* or *China Week* once a year) rather than embedded

■ when a school rushes in a new initiative to satisfy an Ofsted inspection

■ where activities focus on celebrating a culture but ignore the hard issues of attitudes and racism

■ if initiatives are imposed by senior staff while most teachers don't share an antiracist ethos

A whole-school approach to antiracism will also be tokenistic if, for example, lunchtime supervisors don't know how to report or challenge racist incidents, or if the school's race equality policy is not translated into classroom practice because teachers feel they have already covered it through one-off activities. Tokenism occurs when activities emphasise exotic differences in cultures by taking a tourist approach to diversity. It might be characterised by a school that occasionally covers other cultures through topics using displays, visitors,

festival cooking or creative arts and multicultural weeks, and then returns to regular classroom activities which acknowledge only the dominant culture.

To avoid tokenism the experiences provided throughout the school need to focus on shared human needs and experiences, rather than following an 'us and them' approach. Essentially, antiracist issues need to permeate the curriculum, with an emphasis on people having more similarities than differences. An example is the language we use. If we say '*they* have mosques like *we* have churches'; '*they* celebrate Divali like *we* celebrate Christmas'; '*they* live in caravans like *we* live in houses'; or '*they* eat chappatis like *we* eat bread' we are identifying groups as 'us' and 'them'. It is better practice to say '*some* people live in caravans and some in houses' or '*some* people worship in mosques and *others* in churches'. We need to avoid language which suggests that 'our' views are the norm against which other ways of life are judged.

Token changes of content will not lead to quality antiracist education. Antiracist education is about attitudes and relationships, about people everywhere having much in common; it is not a pack of materials.

Section 2 illustrates how a whole-school approach can be initiated and developed, and in each example considers the role of some pivotal activities within the working methods of the school.

■ 2.1: Whole-school approach ... starting from a Healthy Schools Policy

This is the approach taken by a nursery and infant school in a Lake District village with 200 pupils. At the time there were four children in the school whose origins were in other countries.

This school places its race equality objectives within the framework of a Healthy Schools Policy. It has developed the ethos that race awareness is part of being a healthy person, and within this framework has run a series of multicultural weeks that were not isolated incidents but part of an all-round experience for pupils. A sub-committee of staff and governors consulted with all staff and parents to develop the policy, adding a section on values, based on the school's ethos. Another section entitled *Gifts to the children* was the result of a powerful exercise involving staff, governors, parents and pupils. It focused on the core skills and attitudes the whole school wanted to work towards.

The school uses its Healthy Schools Policy to ensure the inclusion of antiracist and multicultural education at whole-school level, an essential part of developing healthy minds in children and staff alike. In this way, antiracist education has been placed at the core of the school's work rather than on the periphery.

Healthy Schools Policy Introduction

The areas covered by this policy include health education, sex and relationships education, citizenship, drug education, race equality, health and safety and personal and social development. It draws together different strands that underpin an understanding of how to live our daily lives within the community in a healthy way. This document is a statement of the aims, principles and strategies for teaching and learning in all of these areas.

The policy includes sections on attitudes and values, gifts to the children that the whole school has agreed that we aim to give to children, and strategies for teaching and learning, resources, ethos statement, performance management and monitoring and evaluation.

The school's multicultural work is part of an holistic approach which recognises that if pupils can talk about themselves in a healthy way they will have a firm basis from which to empathise with and respect others. The ethos is 'having respect and value for other people's religions, faiths and cultures, whilst not being apologetic about our own'. All aspects of a pupil's social development are considered within this framework. The school also uses thinking skills and

Personal and social skills, knowledge, attitudes and understanding

Gifts to the children

Governors, staff, parents and pupils have agreed that we aim to gift the children with:

A sense of humour; health; to be polite; self esteem; independence; curiosity; enthusiasm; to always be kind and considerate; a love of exercise; knowledge; discipline and respect; confidence; kindness and to think of others; respectfulness; work ethos; able to listen to others and themselves; security; happiness; a love of the arts; to always try your best; friendliness; self belief; a love of food; to be able to share and take turns; to feel loved and to give love; positive attitude; tolerance; confidence to take responsibility; a love of life.

enquiry methods (such as Philosophy for Children, described in section 4.3) to help pupils reflect on their ideas and actions. This is particularly valuable in the context of behaviours and attitudes towards others.

Reaching the whole school community

Addressing all aspects of the Healthy Schools Policy is an ongoing process that is relevant to governors, staff, parents and pupils, and to partners in the school's Networked Learning Community. The headteacher continually seeks practical ways to engage all the staff. For example she includes agenda items at staff meetings on multicultural choices in the context of ordering resources, and this has had practical results in choosing a new supplier for jigsaws.

The school strives to raise awareness in parents and the wider community so pupils are not in the awkward position of hearing one message at school and a different one at home. This is challenging and despite making continuous efforts to involve parents and community groups, it is not always successful.

Pivotal activities within the whole-school approach: multicultural arts events

The school organised one year's work to include two multicultural arts focuses, one on China and one on the Caribbean. Each 'art week' was spread over a school term, ensuring greater depth of work. This timescale was decided after reviewing previous cultural events that had taken place over only one intensive week.

We plan to use artists who bring their cultures into our school in a very exciting and positive way. Albie, to represent the African-Caribbean culture, and Chinese people from the local community and beyond will be working with the children. There will be opportunities for the artists to talk to the children on a personal level about themselves.

The project we are planning will be expensive so we are bidding for money to help us to provide a valuable, lasting experience for the children and the adults involved. Staff are involved in training so they continue to deliver aspects of these experiences as normal practice in our school. Appropriate resources will be purchased. The project is promoting such a buzz amongst everyone; the motivation is certainly there! We still talk with excitement about the lasting benefits of our last residency. Through involving parents and the local community we anticipate that there will be a greater understanding of the positive aspects of cultural diversity.

Extract from a funding bid written by a governor

Chinese arts focus

In preparation, some assemblies and classwork introduced aspects of Chinese culture. Characters from the Chinese New Year story were explored and the role play areas were turned into a Chinese restaurant. Parents were involved in cooking and tasting some Chinese food. A range of displays including artwork and lantern-making were prominent around school.

The China project culminated with a week on Chinese New Year which included artists, dancers and calligraphers. Children produced dance and artwork inspired by the animals associated with the Chinese years. They made opera masks and practised Chinese script. Some of the artists worked in nursery and Foundation Stage classes and others in KS1, so all pupils throughout the school shared in the experience with a variety of activities across all curriculum areas.

All the teachers were encouraged to dip in and out of the project rather than deliver it all at once. This helped the staff to develop better personal knowledge of China. The school plans to build the Chinese topic into the curriculum so that the learning from this project can be revisited annually.

Caribbean arts focus

The artist Albie Ollivierre worked in school for two weeks, primarily on dance. Albie is a professional choreographer and dance tutor. He combines different art forms and dance styles including African-Caribbean, urban, jazz, R&B and contemporary. Albie made it clear to pupils that he was a Londoner who had roots in the Caribbean. Pupils explored aspects of Caribbean life by locating the various islands on a globe, and visiting the role play area made into a Caribbean home.

Albie's sessions with each class included an introduction, a warm up, and a dance routine through which the children could experience different styles, movements and music from African-Caribbean related traditions. The activities used rhythm, voice, mime, movement, images or games and created a sense of enjoyment and spontaneity. The class teachers, teaching assistants and other carers joined in. Thanks to this residency, a long-term dance exhibition was displayed in school and a number of the dance routines and rhythms have been put into regular PE sessions.

Future activities

The school followed up the arts activities by using persona dolls (see Section 4.8) so that pupils and teachers could address some of the more complex issues relating to ethnic minority communities in Britain. The dolls help pupils to realise that Chinese people don't live only in China and black people don't live only in Africa or the Caribbean.

The school negotiated with members of their local Women's Institute to make four persona dolls to add to the two

Display produced as part of China arts week

Display produced as part of African-Caribbean dance project with the artist Albie Ollivierre

I liked listening Mary talking Chinese it was different

I have never seen a Chinese person before it was nice to see one

I liked my name that you made in Chinese. I thought the Chinese Writing was ace

She taught us about China. She showed us about colours on masks and let us know about he characters.

I liked Mary's hair. She was pretty. I liked her voice when she was speaking Chinese. She was friendly

I love Mary because she lets us try things like speaking Chinese. She taught us some Chinese like Monkey King

We had lots of fun eating with chopsticks. We got lots of rice on the floor. Chinese people must be very clever

I never knew I liked spring rolls

I liked using chopsticks

I didn't know China was so big

We wrote Chinese when we took the order for food in our Chinese Restaurant

We read the menus to choose Chinese food. We tasted lots of different food like spring rolls, seaweed rice and sweet and sour

already purchased. With the help of training by an advisory teacher, a persona for each doll has been created. Personas have been chosen to ensure that children can find something in each of the dolls to identify with, such as a favourite toy or having a baby at home. Regular use of the persona dolls is helping pupils to build on what they learned about China and the Caribbean, and to apply this learning to the ways they relate to other children who they perceive to be different.

Outcomes

This project shows a subtle shift from multicultural education towards antiracist education. The headteacher has introduced some discussion activities about race and racism in staff meetings, as she recognises that achieving a level of acceptance and acknowledgement amongst all staff is essential to introducing antiracist education across the school curriculum. It is an ongoing process that will be developed over coming years.

> *In some ways it is easier to address race issues about Black people in our community, but it is still a challenge to introduce discussion on Travellers, who I think would face racism in this community. While members of staff and hopefully parents are moving away from being stereotypical about Black people, this sadly isn't true of their attitudes to Travellers.*
>
> Headteacher

■ 2.2: Whole-school approach ... based on progression through the school

This is the approach taken by an urban junior school with over 300 pupils on role. The whole-school ethos embraces a range of activities including Philosophy for Children and forum theatre (see sections 4.1 and 4.3). Training sessions are for the whole school not just teaching staff. The school raises the profile and impact of its work by leading joint activities with other schools in its Network Learning Community. Progression is central to all activities. The school has a defined approach to thinking, questioning and sharing values. Problematic incidents are often highlighted in assemblies and related issues are then followed up in each class.

The original motivation for the development of this whole-school approach towards antiracist education was as a direct response to the ongoing background of rivalry and gang-style behaviour in the local community. This

> *Ours is a way of working, an outlet. Individual activities sit in the context of a wider multi-year development programme. And really school isn't the only place to tackle attitudes. It is outside; the chatter that you hear in the hairdressers, in the pub, in the community. And it is not the end result that matters most, but the process that you go through.*
>
> Headteacher

rivalry has not been related to ethnicity but represents a significant and destructive clash of cultures, in particular between pupils from neighbouring schools.

Despite these problems there is a strong sense of community in the school. The small numbers of black and ethnic minority pupils have been well accepted, partly because they have been articulate, sociable and able to respond positively to other pupils. By contrast, some children who have joined the school from a different UK community, or from a different part of the town, have not always been well accepted. This may be related to the tribal divisions mentioned above, which mean that some children are less willingly accepted into the dominant school community, sometimes because their responses show an intention to retain their existing cultural identity.

Whole staff involvement

The whole staff, including governors and support staff such as lunchtime assistants, took part in training sessions led by an advisory teacher to ensure that everyone shared a common vocabulary on antiracist education. A range of projects and classroom activities were planned within the curriculum, to fit within the school's existing use of methodologies such as philosophical enquiry and circle time. Any single activity was seen within the context of a wider whole-school approach and not as a stand-alone activity.

Challenging incidents as they arise

The teachers want pupils to develop skills that help them consider and review their attitudes, think for themselves and question what they hear, whether in the curriculum, during break-times or in response to incidents. The aim is to challenge pupils' thinking and encourage them to think beyond their own personal wants and needs.

For example, the school day might begin with an assembly reflecting on an incident that took place the previous day. The title 'A new way of thinking about an old problem' might be used to introduce any topic that arises in this way. Class teachers take the topic forwards from the assembly into their classroom, in order to address the underlying issues. In one example, an incident between pupils was highlighted and all the pupils were asked to consider whether this was a bullying problem or an incident between friends, a discussion that continued in circle time and philosophy sessions over the following days. On other occasions the focus of assembly might be newspaper articles about incidents involving children worldwide.

Drama role-plays

Pivotal elements of this school's approach include a progression of drama-based activities:

■ *Everybody's Different* in Year 4 (focusing on respecting difference)

■ *Choices* in Year 5 (focusing on peer pressure in relation to drug use)

■ *Losing Face* in Year 6 (focusing on strategies to deal with peer pressure in general)

All three dramas are fundamentally about peer pressure. The progression approach helps pupils build understanding and learn to take responsibility for their actions. Though each could stand alone, they are stronger through being part of the whole-school ethos. The dramas all contain elements of skills development, but 'you have to make sure the message isn't lost in developing the skills' (headteacher).

The sessions are led by the headteacher in strong dramatic style, which is memorable and fun. They are and followed up by class teachers to ensure that reflection on key issues takes place at classroom level across the school, with the central emphasis on pupils learning to question, to listen to one another, and to think for themselves. The dramas have also been facilitated by the headteachers of other schools in the Network Learning Community, which means that pupils from different feeder schools transferring to local secondary schools will have had similar experiences and shared the message.

Choices

Choices is a drama for Year 5 pupils that focuses on peer pressure in relation to drug use. It is vital for the school to tackle this topic because a number of pupils live with drug problems in their families. For example, one boy was taken into care as an infant, largely because of his mother's drug addiction, and has only just been allowed to live at home again.

When presenting this drama, it is important that drug users are not condemned or judged. Pupils who are affected by drug use at home mustn't feel alienated, nor that their family and friends are being criticised. Instead, drug use is presented as a personal choice with certain consequences, and it is made clear that even if someone wants to change their choice, it may be too late if they become addicted.

The session begins with a class discussion to introduce the issues and to learn part of the song. The pupils then work on the drama in three groups: The Good Gang; The Lazy Gang; and The Pushers. Each group is led by a teacher in a separate room, so they don't know what the other groups are doing. They all follow the same outline which involves building the plot for the drama and working in freeze-frame (action takes place then freezes while action takes place in another part of the group). They find solutions to the problems identified when building the plot. The class then comes back together for full rehearsals, ready to perform the show to the rest of the school. A whole class reflection closes the session. The issue of making choices is applied to various other contexts, such as racist behaviour.

Outcomes

One child in this class has long-term family problems through drug use. It is hard for him to get through any session without becoming loud and disruptive. Normally he attends part time, but during this activity he was highly engaged. So much so, his support worker had little to do all day, and the school arranged for him to stay through the afternoon as he took a lead role in one of the groups.

The Lazy Gang rap

■ 2.3: Whole-school approach ... through an underlying curriculum

This is the approach taken by a rural primary school with 40 pupils on role. After an in-service training day for the staff and governors by an advisory teacher, and attendance by the headteacher at several multicultural and antiracist courses, the school was keen to achieve a whole-school approach to antiracist education.

The staff looked through their existing curriculum plans to identify activities, units and projects already happening or planned that could contribute to delivering their race equality objectives. A range of curriculum units and special projects were identified which would help pupils of all ages explore issues of diversity and these were drawn together into an *Underlying Curriculum Action Plan.*

Pivotal activities of the whole school approach – linking with a school in Manchester

As part of the preparation for a visit from pupils from the Manchester school, the Cumbrian pupils considered and agreed what they would need to tell the visitors about the Lake District environment. They discussed what they thought it would be like in Manchester and assumed that violence and drugs would dominate city life. While it is true that parts of Manchester are more violent than the

I wanted our pupils to interact with children from an urban environment and ethnically diverse family backgrounds, and to do so in an everyday school-based way. I was keen for us to be able to go to the city. Because I was looking for it to happen I was able to latch onto certain channels, such as the British Mountaineering Council Visitor Payback Scheme.

I'm really glad, as a small school, that they visited us first. The city children had a confidence to tackle new experiences that ours don't have because they have such different life experiences to draw on. Now that the link is real and meaningful the children are very positive about going to Manchester to see what happens at lunchtime and playtime in the school and it is these everyday things that interest our children the most.
Headteacher

Lake District, the pupils living in Manchester didn't perceive their neighbourhood as violent and were proud of their home town.

During the visit to Cumbria, funded partly by the British Mountaineering Council and the Lake District National Park Authority, some of the Manchester pupils encountered sheep for the first time and enjoyed being on the fells rather than in

the shops. They took part in shared outdoor education work and a day of team-building activities, and these shared experiences ensured that the Manchester pupils did not feel like tourists, and that the Cumbrian pupils did not feel like exhibits in a zoo.

As part of the preparation for a return visit to Manchester nearly a year later:

■ pupils were given a camera to take take a photograph of their house, to send to the other school in advance of the visit

■ pupils reflected on where they lived and discussed ways the Cumbrian and Manchester environments differ or are similar

■ pupils in Manchester discussed 'what it means to be a child in Manchester'

The Cumbrian pupils made a reciprocal trip to Manchester to explore life in the city. The Manchester school has 400 pupils, so the school sizes and staff/pupil ratios are quite different. The contrasts the children noticed were that Manchester is bustling, busy and commercial, while their village is serene and beautiful and full of tourists. Even with much preparation, it was initially a culture shock for the Cumbrian pupils coming from their traditionally white monolingual community to experience the Manchester community where over 40 languages are spoken and the residents originate in more than 30 nations.

Diversity and inclusion are buzz words at the moment. The pupils at both schools have learned a lot from each other, as did the staff. School linking is easy to think up, but harder to sustain. Start-up funding at the beginning really helps, as does a personal contact within each school. I already knew the headteacher in Manchester and both schools have a shared vision to work in this way.

We are all keen for the linking to continue, through email contact and a shared art project. What has kept it working and manageable has been the reliance on real human contact. Our next step is to link with an Indian school for street children because of personal contact through the chair of our PTA and the village GP.
Headteacher

Some questions asked by Manchester pupils when they visited Cumbria

Where are the shops?

Have you ever been on a motorway?

How do you manage in a school this small?

How do the teachers teach you when you're all different ages?

Do you have the same money here?

What do you do in the evening?

Some questions asked by Cumbrian pupils when they visited Manchester

Why aren't you having lunch with us? (some were fasting for Ramadan)

Why is half of the school lunch menu halal?

Don't you know all the kids in your school?

Outcomes

Before the link took place, one of the school governors said, 'I really don't want it to be about funny people wearing funny hats doing funny things. I want it to be about real people doing real things in real places.' The motivation was to form relationships and to get to know something about people's lives, not labouring the issues but letting them develop naturally.

The issues that emerged through this project have not been about race, despite the obvious differences in ethnic make-up, but about the pupils' perceptions of rural and urban environments. Parents have been supportive. They understand that the pupils need opportunities to experience a wider view of contemporary Britain and they appreciate the school's role in providing this. Pupils were excited to have the opportunity to experience what other schools are like and how other people live their lives.

Pupils sharing outdoor activities, photographer Charlie Hedley

Wall display produced to share learning in the school's project work

Embedding diversity issues into regular classroom work

The staff are finding ways to adapt and develop curriculum units, for example when teaching about the Tudors they use a teaching pack *Africans in Tudor Britain* produced by the Ethnic Minority Achievement Service in Lancashire. Special projects offered by Cumbria Education Service are enthusiastically taken up, including the use of persona dolls and pupil participation in *Ally Comes to Cumbria* and *Fortress Europe* (see sections 4.1 and 4.2).

In the context of a topic on *Homes and Houses* the infant class borrowed a Traveller home corner from the Traveller education team within the Specialist Advisory Teaching Service. The pupils enjoyed playing in the trailer and parents were happy about it. The school wanted to tackle the local community's tendency to be hostile to, or dislike, 'off-comers'. What became clear through talking with parents was that the issue of Travellers is less contentious in this community than elsewhere in Cumbria. Here it is tourists and second-home owners that arouse greatest resentment.

Underlying Curriculum Action Plan

Targets	Training and staff development/ resources required	Success criteria
Carry out an audit of resources, policies and books	Attend Cumbria Education Service course – *Activities to combat Prejudice and Racism at KS1 and 2.*	Update of action plan based on Cumbria Education Service guidance
	Attend Early Years Global Education Workshop, CDEC	Agreement of governors and staff about action plan
Create a bank of practical activities to use in our predominantly white school	Attend Cumbria Education Service courses e.g. *Coming Unstuck; Persona Dolls*	List of materials created and distributed amongst staff
	Pupils attend Cumbria Education Service sponsored *Fortress Europe* and *Ally Comes to Cumbria.*	Monitoring of teaching and planning shows materials being used
Examine the use of positive images in literacy, story, and art that support and acknowledge the difference and variety in contemporary Britain	Books, photos, texts, music, websites	List of texts and resources created and distributed amongst staff
		Monitoring of teaching and planning shows books and resources being used
Purchase additional materials, resources and books to support this		
		Heightened awareness of prejudice and racist attitudes and language amongst school community
Explore what prejudice and racism there is amongst staff and children	3 x circle time sessions 1 x staff meeting	
		Anti-racist policy validated by governors
Create an antiracist policy that demonstrates our commitment to antiracist policies, with a statement to be included in all our other policies	1 x staff meeting In-service training from advisory teacher	
		Half-termly programme of exchange activities planned and taking place, including a visit to Manchester
Create a strong positive link with our partner school in Manchester to be supported by email, letters and visits	Coach journey Create a programme of exchange activities for all children to carry out	
		Manchester children to visit us as part of their residential experience
Update all policies with an antiracism statement	1 x secretarial day	All policies have an antiracist statement
Review our practice against Cumbria Education Service guidelines to identify good antiracist education and avoid tokenism	1 x staff meeting and 1 x curriculum meeting Attendance at courses	Identification of areas of concern, and carry out actions identified in audit to update policy

■ 2.4: Whole-school approach ... through multi-school art projects

This is the approach taken by a village primary school with fewer than 40 pupils. The school's location in a village popular with visitors means it is inundated with requests to visit. To the headteacher this can feel as though it is seen as a rare and interesting exhibit in a zoo. Yet children in this village experience rural isolation because they don't have access to mainstream activities such as Brownies, youth clubs, discos or bowling alleys. Many pupils reflect the views of the local community towards outsiders, views which can be closed and prone to stereotyping. To counteract this the teachers use investigative projects and thinking skills methodologies such as Philosophy for Children.

All teaching staff and governors attended a one-day conference on Race Equality organised by Cumbria Education Service.

Poster produced for
Paint Race Positively

This became the catalyst for developing an ambitious multi-school art project, *Paint Race Positively*, designed to focus on racism.

With the support of the headteacher, one of the governors took responsibility for raising funds and organising a programme of activities reflecting *Paint Race Positively*. The aims were:

■ to provide a platform for children to nurture their talents

■ to showcase the excellence of small schools

■ to highlight diversity and inclusion through extra- and cross-curricular activities in an essentially rural and monocultural area

Pupils started by looking at pictures of West Africa and identifying characteristics that showed similarities and differences to Cumbria. They participated in a dance project where they froze in certain poses and took photographs of the poses which showed people in positive relationships. They used an IT package to make artistic pictures out of these photos. During the lead up to the festival children learned about Martin Luther King, Anne Frank, and Stephen Lawrence. They participated in the forum theatre production of *Ally Comes to Cumbria* and this enabled them to discuss some hard-hitting concepts about racism (see section 4.1).

Poster Competition

The governor invited 72 small schools to take part in the *Paint Race Positively* arts festival and competition. Pupils were asked to produce an imaginative A4 poster celebrating the ethnic diversity of multicultural Britain, using paint, collage, decoupage, pastels or IT. 268 posters were submitted from primary schools across Cumbria and the artwork was judged by a local artist, local hoteliers, and the Chair of the Cumbria branch of UNISON. Local residents and businesses donated the prizes.

Paint Race Positively opened with the artwork beautifully displayed at the local village hall. Dignitaries and pupils and teachers from participating schools attended the launch and awards were given out by Jack Mapanje, a human rights activist and poet-in-residence at the Wordsworth Trust. He worked with pupils and read his poem ending: 'if you must paint, paint race positively'. The Chair of Cumbria branch of UNISON talked about his childhood experiences of racism in Cumbria, and he recalled sitting in the bath as an eight-year-old, scrubbing himself to try to make his skin white.

Children can make a difference, they are the future and they can stamp out racism.

Chair of Cumbria branch of UNISON

Because the village is so popular with tourists, people from many places visited *Paint Race Positively*. The artwork has since been displayed at several presentations and conferences throughout Cumbria and was used in the school calendar.

Paint Race Positively workshops

The second week of the festival was musical. Workshops were offered to participating schools featuring music from a range of cultures by different artists, and workshops for orchestra, choir and percussion. A Bharat Natayam dancer worked with pupils on a dance performance and told stories from the Hindu tradition. Pupils enjoyed salsa dancing and playing a Javanese gamelan. Musicians worked with the pupils on a large-scale piece highlighting diversity through various musical genres, including orchestral music, choir and a large-scale percussion ensemble. This culminated in a festival concert at the packed village hall, with prizes awarded to the most improved musician and voice of the week. Feet were set tapping to worldwide rhythms.

> *It's extremely important that children are taught to respect each other and to value each other's culture and background. Tolerance isn't enough, it has to be much more than that.* Headteacher

Outcomes

The school established a link with a school of the same name in Hackney in London and its pupils submitted pictures for *Paint Race Positively*. These pictures, with war images and caricatures, showed sophisticated political intelligence.

Building on *Paint Race Positively*, the school organised a week-long multi-school arts festival the following year to celebrate the diversity of cultures within Cumbria. *Tradcraft* celebrated different local traditions and illustrated how nearly-forgotten crafts and skills can be fostered as a means of communicating the diverse heritage found in the county.

Tradcraft helped pupils understand that diversity is not just about people of different ethnicities. It included an art competition open to all 128 small schools in Cumbria, and workshops on poetry-writing, story-telling, spinning, weaving, long-stitch tapestry, rush-bearing, traditional musical instruments and clog-dancing. At the end of the week an art exhibition at the village hall showcased all the entries to the competition and during a ceilidh, youngsters from several small schools demonstrated some of the skills they had learned.

A third multi-school arts project is planned. *World Wide Web* will continue the theme of diversity, placing the village at the centre of a world wide web, and

Pupil's painting submitted to Paint Race Positively.

tracing visitors' paths to and from the village. It will link participating schools with villages as remote and diverse as New Zealand, Japan, Mongolia, Canada, as well as European and African towns. The aim is to get to know some of these people, their places and values, through workshops and a concert of music, song, dance, dress and food, plus an exhibition of artwork and artefacts with video and audiotapes of the stories.

We are celebrating Cumbrian cultures and traditions and appreciating that from west Cumbria to north Cumbria traditions will be different and cultures may be different. We want to show children that you don't only need to look to another country or to someone of a different ethnic origin to learn from a different culture. Headteacher

■ 2.5: Whole school approach ... involving the whole school community

We work from the belief that everybody has something to share, including the community. It takes a whole village to raise a child.
Headteacher

This is the approach taken by a two-class village school with fewer than 40 pupils, catering for Reception to Year 3. The school places strong emphasis on respect for each child's individuality. The values that underpin the school's approach to teaching and learning reflect the importance given to diversity, in particular that everyone's contribution is important.

Ethos statement
- We believe that children are at the heart of the local community and that every person in the community has a role to play in the education of children
- Each child is valued and treated as an individual
- Our school is the centre for learning within the community. We are a community of life-long learners supporting and learning from each other

Putting principles into practice
1. Community involvement in the school

This is a community school. Community members are involved in classes and pupils regularly visit community-based groups as part of their learning. Community involvement strengthens the curriculum and adds to the diversity of the school. Some of the children live in remote rural places and may have little opportunity to communicate with people except at school.

Input by members of the community is built into planning across the school and is a regular feature of the school day. For example:

- the clerk to the governors gives spinning and weaving demonstrations
- a local beekeeper gives demonstrations as part of the science curriculum
- a local resident who is a retired industry worker regularly helps in the classroom
- a local artist who has a child at the school helps deliver the art curriculum
- local journalists come into school to contribute to a topic on media
- local builders give demonstrations on construction, and the pupils then work with large interlocking bricks

■ a local plant-machinery company have brought diggers and dumpers onto the school grounds for pupils to investigate

■ the funding bid for the newly-built nursery was made by members of the community and is community-managed and run

---

Every day between 8.50am and 9.10am it is like a free-for-all in here with mums, children, babies, buggies and the rest of it.

It might seem like chaos but this is a crucial part of communication between the school and parents and it leads to the high level of parental involvement in school that we have today.

The parents feel important because they are so welcomed in the school at this time. This is also when they can meet and communicate with each other, another key aspect of building community strength in this locality.

It is very important that the staff don't give the impression that they are too busy for the parents, as this will undermine any confidence they might have in offering their support in the classroom. Furthermore, it means that potential issues and problems can be raised and chatted over in a comfortable environment and thus major issues are identified and dealt with early. Headteacher

---

Tips for involving the community in school

The school has built its relationship with community members over many years, keeping an open door policy and ensuring that the school is welcoming to all. The following are particularly important:

■ The school must be welcoming to parents and others in the community as soon as they walk onto the premises. The headteacher should not use her power and position as headteacher to create a threatening atmosphere

■ The headteacher and staff should spend time talking to people to find out whether and how they can contribute in school.

■ Anyone who is nervous about going into school should be given support and encouragement.

■ The parents of nursery or reception children, who are often keen to get involved in the life of the school, need to receive a strong message of welcome and a clear idea of concrete ways to participate in classroom life.

■ Not all parents or members of the community see themselves as having a specific practical skill or knowledge area to offer. Teachers need to give a clear message that everyone can make a contribution, so that people feel more confident about putting themselves forward.

Parents often become interested in school projects and ask to participate. For example, some saw what pupils were doing in their art classes with the local artist, so by popular demand an out-of-school art class was arranged for adults. At the end of this project the work by both children and adults was displayed at an art exhibition, giving a powerful message about life-long learning, and the understanding that learning doesn't end at the school gates.

Going out into the community

Pupils visited a local food company to learn about sandwich making. Back in school the pupils set up a sandwich factory, culminating in a visit to school by the Managing Director to see what the pupils had done and to taste some of their sandwich creations.

One pupil organised a wedding as part of her self-directed learning

2. Valuing children as individuals – an open session in the weekly timetable

The school works to an individualised learning programme for each pupil. A subject-specialist teaching model is used so staff teach across the school rather than one teacher per class. This means that staff members know each pupil's individual needs and strengths.

All pupils have open sessions in their weekly timetable for at least half a day, during which they initiate their own learning. This has been a regular feature of the curriculum for many years, beginning as a process of plan-do-review and becoming more sophisticated. Pupils use this time to work on projects that reflect their own interests. For example one child decided to organise a wedding. She agreed who would be married, organised invitations, made clothes, and arranged a venue and a vicar. She brought knowledge of cultural issues to this project that she had learned outside the classroom. Other ideas for individual projects have included forming pop groups, writing plays, starting new clubs, and making a Bond film.

Planning

At the beginning of each week the whole class sits together and each pupil talks in turn about their plans for the week. The other pupils ask questions for clarification, and this helps them build these plans. For example in the wedding project the others asked questions such as, 'How will you decide who to marry?' The thinking and questioning skills developed through the school's use of philosophical enquiry have enabled pupils to support each other and develop their thinking through these planning sessions.

Doing

The pupils implement their plans, a busy process in the classroom which has a good deal of output.

Reviewing

At the end of the week all the pupils are divided into small review groups. Pupils talk about their work, then other pupils ask questions such as, 'Where did the idea come from?', 'How did you do it?', 'Would it be better if …?' This review process supports and values each pupil's work and helps them plan for the next stage. The projects often carry on for many weeks. The quality of numeracy and literacy in their work is impressive: for example, three pupils who formed the Animal Crazy Club wrote and sent out a letter to parents in the style of the head's letters.

This process empowers pupils by giving them control over the content of their learning, something that can make some teachers feel uncomfortable. Hence the challenge is for the teacher to feel comfortable about handing over power to the pupils. These projects are examples of meaningful, purposeful learning, during which pupils are highly motivated so they achieve at a very high level.

> *Our children are very good at giving or taking positive criticism. They have learned to say things to each other without taking offence, and they can move each other's thinking on, even if just to say they disagree with someone else's suggestions.*
> Headteacher

3. Philosophy for Children

Pupils are encouraged to learn from each other and their ideas and interests are highly valued. This is reflected in the regular use of philosophical enquiry methodologies (see section 4.3), once a week in the Year 2/3 class, and regularly in the Reception/Y1 class.

RE and collective worship are also times when children share their thoughts and develop and extend their thinking through listening and responding to others. Pupils might respond to a given question, such as 'What makes a good school?'. They are encouraged to agree or disagree and explain their reasoning. The older children support the younger children and illustrate how these skills can be used in dialogue of this kind. Parents often comment on the value of these enquires.

4. Input on Islam

As a role play area, teachers made an Islamic home. They went to Bradford and bought a Qu'ran stand, salwar kameez and other clothes and artefacts and taught the children how they are used. This is now embedded in the RE curriculum as part of the study of Islam.

While she was dining at the nearest Bangladeshi restaurant, the headteacher persuaded the proprietor to come into school to talk about being a Muslim. He came for a half-day so pupils could get to know him, ask questions and hear about his culture and values in a non-threatening and informal way. This man wasn't a practising Muslim, so pupils learned that not all Muslims are devout or wear beards. And when teachers visited their link school in Tower Hamlets they found that the mosque was reached via doors under the railway bridge, which helped challenge the stereotyped image of the mosque as a grand building with minarets and a dome.

Section 3
How do we build on community issues and school situations?

Some teachers focus on antiracist issues by building on situations within school and they take this further by exploring ways to share the learning with parents and the wider community. Schools certainly have a role in educating parents, governors and the wider community about bullying driven by prejudice.

To be effective, multicultural and antiracist education must be grounded in the real issues which affect schools in their own communities. Teachers should recognise the prejudice that exists against pupils from different estates or from neighbouring towns, and that prejudice of this kind can be as destructive as racism. Teaching methods associated with delivering multicultural and antiracist education are equally relevant in addressing local tensions. Local issues can be a useful starting point for introducing and addressing the national and global issues that teachers, parents and pupils may only have experienced through the media.

Section 3 shows how schools have introduced aspects of antiracist education as a response to incidents and situations in their own school and community within the framework of whole-school curriculum development. The message that diversity is the norm can then spread beyond the classroom. Some schools have used curriculum-based topics to produce eye-catching displays on view to parents and visitors. The delivery of some programmes has been made more successful by bringing together pupils from different schools and a range of wider community links is illustrated throughout many of our case studies.

Dear members of the WI,

I am writing to request your help with the multicultural work that we do in school.

To help our young pupils begin to develop empathy and to know about people from other cultures we have purchased two persona rag dolls; an African-Caribbean boy and a Chinese girl. These dolls are quite large and cost £60 each.

We would like to extend this resource by inviting your talented members, who may be interested in sewing, to make us some more dolls so that we can use them in all our classrooms to tackle prejudicial attitudes.

There are 260 pupils in school so we would like to have more than two dolls - for instance a Muslim girl, a Gypsy boy, and a Jewish girl and a Nigerian boy.

We would of course pay for all materials. We can lend you our existing dolls so you can see how they are made.

I hope that your members are able to help us with this exciting project and look forward to hearing from you soon.

Yours sincerely

■ 3.1: Dealing with racist incidents

Some governors, teachers and parents in mainly white schools are still saying that work on prejudice and discrimination doesn't have a high priority because, 'we don't have any of them (Black, Asian or Travellers) in our school'. These schools are adopting a colour-blind approach. They believe that the colour of a child's skin is irrelevant because, 'they are all children and I treat all children alike'. But children require treatment that reflects their individual background, personality, capabilities and needs. Treating them all the same fails to acknowledge their differences, denies their identity and does not allow all to have an equal chance. Children should be treated equally but not the same.

What is a racist incident?

A racist incident is any incident which is perceived to be racist by the victim or any other person. It may be perpetrated against individuals on the basis of their race, colour, nationality, culture, language or religion.

Stephen Lawrence Enquiry Report (Macpherson 1999)

Teachers in mainly white schools may not have daily evidence of racist behaviour but any unconscious prejudice is likely to become more overt once an outsider or potential victim is present. If there is no-one there to be the victim of racist attitudes, it will appear that racism doesn't exist. Teachers have been heard to say, 'We had no trouble with racism until a Traveller came to school' as if the child is to blame for the prejudice her presence exposes.

Racism may manifest because children assume that the culture they are most familiar with is the only one that matters. When they meet someone who has a different culture they may become more aware of their own culture but unless they understand that both are part of a larger picture, racism in the form of cultural domination may be perpetuated.

Even though it is a statutory requirement for schools to report racist incidents to the LEA, some headteachers don't send in reports, because they think admitting to racist incidents will reflect badly on their school.

In some cases an antiracist awareness-raising programme can generate an increase in racist incident reports, and this is a positive outcome. Many incidents take place during playtimes and will only be reported if they are recognised as racist and considered

---

A nursery and infant school decided to focus attention on tackling prejudice through its Healthy Schools Policy, because staff felt that the ability to form good relationships was part of developing a healthy mind. Part of its multicultural programme was a collapsed curriculum-intensive culture week of activities based on Chinese New Year.

Shortly afterwards a midday supervisor reported a racist incident in the playground, when a pupil from the neighbouring junior school shouted abuse to a Chinese pupil through the fence. It is quite likely that this incident would not have been included in the school's racist incident monitoring report had the lunchtime staff not been included in whole-staff training on antiracist issues.

---

serious enough to report by a child or supervising adult. If midday supervisors and school support staff are included in whole-school training they may begin to notice incidents they previously ignored and begin to report them as racist name-calling.

Don't ignore racist comments. If they are made by adults or older children our response might be:

"I'm sorry you think that. It's not my experience."
"I don't agree with you. What makes you think that?"
"Please don't include me in that. What makes you say that?"

Even with very young children, act sensitively and promptly. Take it seriously, don't just make a casual comment in response, and don't side-step the issues. Embarrassed comments to the perpetrator such as, "You shouldn't say that," or to the victim, "Try to forget it," are inappropriate. Make it clear to the perpetrator: "Your comment or behaviour was unacceptable, hurtful and is not allowed". Explain fully why this is the case and encourage them to think deeply about it. Don't humiliate them or undermine their self-esteem, or make them feel defensive, because *"Guilt is the glue that keeps prejudice in place"*.

Give pupils correct information about the genetic evidence regarding 'race' that proves there is only one race, the human race. 'Race' is not an appropriate categorisation for people of different cultures.

Any racist incident is a call for action in the curriculum so must be followed up with classroom-based strategies such as circle time, stories, philosophical enquiry and persona doll sessions.

Support the victim and ensure that anyone who overheard the incident understands that it was wrong and unacceptable.

Some Guidelines for Tackling Racism in School

Pupils should know that any racist comments or incidents will be discussed with parents. This makes the school's position clear and may encourage the reinforcement of antiracist practices at home.

Adults in mainly white schools are often concerned about terminology so agreement needs to be reached about what language is appropriate.

Talk through the incident with the perpetrator and the victim and help them settle any parts of their conflict that are unrelated to ethnicity, culture or religion. Explain that there are three main reasons why racist insults are unacceptable:

- they attack a person's family, community and heritage, not just their personality
- they intimidate others, not just the individual under attack
- those who use them believe they are representing widely held views

All pupils, parents, staff and governors need to understand that national laws prohibit racist comments, harassment, graffiti and name-calling in the playground, corridors and toilets as well as in the classroom. Reporting procedures need to be in place, and this must involve the whole staff including administrative, support and lunchtime staff.

If someone at the receiving end of racist insults retaliates, be careful that it is not they who are punished for retaliating, leaving the perpetrator of the original insult feeling free to repeat the offence.

Terminology

Race

Race is a political, not a biological category. Once it was thought that the human species could be divided into separate racial groups based on physical difference but scientists have discredited this idea. The human species shares a common gene pool; only nine genes out of 32,000 determine skin colour. Studies of DNA have proved that there is much more genetic variation within each so-called racial group than between groups who may look completely different. There are no pure races, yet people still use race as a basis for discrimination.

Black

This term is used to describe all people who may be discriminated against because of their ethnic background. It includes people of African, Caribbean or Asian origin and those with Arab, Cypriot or Latin American backgrounds where skin colour is a determining factor. It is a political definition to unite people of diverse cultures and lifestyles against racism.

Some people use the term Black only for people of African-Caribbean origin. Others prefer the term Brown. Some people with Asian roots call themselves Black but this is usually a political position. Some people prefer to be described by their heritage rather than their skin colour – so 'of African heritage' rather than Black. Most Black and Asian people find the term coloured insulting, outdated and unacceptable. Some Travellers dislike the term Gypsy. Many people with one Black and one white parent would find the term 'half-caste' insulting. 'Mixed-race' is being replaced by 'dual heritage' or 'of mixed parentage'. If in doubt, ask the individual concerned which term they prefer.

If you were part of these conversations, what would you contribute? How would you respond?

How many ethnic minority pupils do you have in school?
Four... what about T...?
I think she's Malaysian.
Then there's B..., but he's no problem.
He told me he's got a new name
"Chinkywog". He thinks it's a great joke.

A 4-year old said in a loud voice,
"Look at that brown lady over there".
The adults in nursery froze with embarrassment, and then one said,
"That's not a nice thing to say".

A group of 8-year-olds were looking at photos that showed Black children playing with white dolls and Lego bricks.
One pupil said to her partner,
"They must be African. Look at the flies on them."

A Black trainee teacher was told by the Headteacher of a school:
"You are Black. We are a middle class area here and there aren't many of your sort around. Do you think you could be happy here?"

A 3-year old told a teacher indignantly:
"Miss, there's no dolls left in the home corner!"
The teacher looked and saw there was a selection of Black dolls, but no white ones.

A 10-year old pupil said to a teacher preparing Chinese food with a small group:
"Miss, look, [pulls eyes sideways and dance up and down] I'm a Chinky Chinaman"

■ 3.2: Responding during circle time to a racist incident

The setting was an urban primary school with nearly 200 pupils. The school had no previous experience of having Traveller pupils on role, while the Traveller children had experience of attending another school in the city and schools in other parts of the country.

A class teacher had observed the Traveller children being bullied in the playground and subjected to aggressive language and insults. The verbal abuse echoed the attitudes of parents and community members. The teacher knew it was important to tackle these attitudes directly with all the pupils to avoid an escalation of anti-Traveller incidents. The Traveller children had not attended school long enough to become established within the class so were prime targets for bullies.

The teacher has a long-standing commitment to global education and was responsible for introducing a programme of awareness about global issues into the school as a result of personal links with Malawi. Her aim is to motivate pupils to take responsibility for global development in their own lives. Tackling racist attitudes and behaviour towards Traveller children was an important element of this process of taking responsibility.

During circle time, with the prior agreement of the Traveller pupils, the teacher asked the class to reflect on the question: 'I wonder what you think a Traveller might be like?' As the children responded in turn around the circle their ideas mirrored a range of common stereotypes.

The teacher asked the three pupils from Traveller families to say whether any of the ideas given by class members were things with which they could identify. They said that statements such as 'Travellers stay in one place for a short time' and 'Travellers don't live in a house' were sometimes true, but needed to be qualified. 'Some of us have got houses, we just move between them.'

The teacher questioned the class further about comments such as 'Travellers are dirty' and explained that this is a frequently used insult. She asked the class to really look at the Traveller pupils and pointed out that they were always extremely clean. She encouraged comments and one Traveller pupil said, 'Yes, it is very important to us to be clean and that everything is clean.'

The teacher told a story about a child in a school who had been told 'You wear glasses, so you have to get out of the room'. She asked the pupils to consider what their feelings were about that. One of the boys who had been abusive to the

Travellers in the playground said 'It's not fair. Because they can't choose if they wear glasses, it just happens to them'. The teacher reminded him that the same is true for people who are born in different places, or who live in different sorts of homes. 'We don't choose to be born to a family who lives in a house. Or to one who doesn't. But we can choose to be respectful to everyone'.

Outcomes

At the end of that day one of the boys who had been abusive came to the class teacher and said, 'I've made friends with Michael [Traveller] and you know, he's really nice'. The teacher felt this signified real progress.

The situation since has been calmer. Two of the boys (one a Traveller and one a former bully) now sit and work together. Pupils in the class have observed this and the teacher hopes that, with constant reinforcement, the others will follow their example and reconsider their own prejudice about children from different backgrounds. There are some particularly challenging pupils in the class who are hard to reach. Their dysfunctional family backgrounds may be the reason for their bullying and racial prejudice. Following the circle time activity most pupils accepted the message and stopped the bullying. The acceptance and understanding shown by the majority of the class is gradually influencing the challenging pupils. They see the others behaving in a reasonable way and are forced to follow suit in order to be accepted by their peers.

Short-term follow-up

The class teacher invited CDEC to lead a philosophical enquiry session using the picture book *Something Else* by Kathryn Cave. Something Else is a lonely creature who does his best to be like others but who is ostracised for being different. He meets a creature even stranger than he is and tries to make friends. When he realises that the stranger is not so different, the two eventually do become friends.

This was the first time the class had taken part in a philosophical enquiry and the method appealed greatly to at least one member of the class, who said: 'I was thinking that I'm different from all my friends, and I didn't know that was part of philosophy'.

After hearing the story the pupils were shown a box and told that inside the box was another *Something Else.* Each child in turn looked inside the box, without showing or telling the others what was there. They saw themselves reflected in a mirror. Pupils discussed the ideas this provoked and generated a range of questions that *Something Else* had made them wonder about:

Why did people leave him out, just because he looks different?
Why is it cruel when the others didn't let Something Else play?
Why did Something Else think that because he is different, they won't let him play?

The pupils voted on which question to enquire into and during the dialogue they quickly moved into considering some of the reasons why someone would want a friend: 'He wanted a friend or he would have been alone'. They discussed whether it was easy or difficult to make a new friend:

When you meet a new person you don't know what their intentions are, if they'll be a friend or be nasty to you. When you come to a new school it's hard to get a new friend because you don't know anyone.

Long-term follow-up

In future sessions the class will go deeper into this topic to consider some of the underlying issues about the ways in which people respond to others whom they see as different. As pupils become more familiar with the enquiry method they feel more confident to give personal examples to illustrate a philosophical point, so they reflect on times they themselves have been unkind to someone or have felt left out because of being different and the moral dilemmas involved.

■ 3.3: Supporting a non-English speaker in school

The setting was an urban infant and nursery school with over 150 pupils. The school received notification that a child would be moving from China with her family and joining the Year 2 class. The headteacher and class teacher considered the suggestions from an ESL specialist teacher about how a Chinese pupil who spoke almost no English could access the whole curriculum while learning English. As the pupil was registered at school well before she arrived in England, the headteacher was able to apply to have support in place for her arrival.

When Chan arrived in school everything was alien to her, not just the language but the style of buildings, the equipment, the pictures, the artwork and people's faces in person and in images. Alongside this culture shock was her loss at moving away from her friends at her previous kindergarten. For the class teacher it was a huge learning curve to work with Chan, ensure she learned English and integrate into the class.

Social integration in the classroom

The school made positive efforts to help Chan integrate socially in her class. All pupils have a learning partner so one was chosen for Chan who wouldn't just tell her all the answers but would help

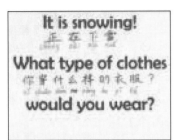

A page from the Dual Language Book, with Mandarin translations

A page from the Dual Language Book, to assist with lieracy teaching.

her to find them out. Jenny interacted well and shared, socially and academically, on a level with Chan. The class teacher reflected: 'It was really super watching Jenny do that with her, and they are still best friends a year on'. The class teacher included Chan in all the daily routines and tasks, such as milk duty and other rotas so that she and the other pupils saw her as a full member of the class.

Home-school partnership

The strong home-school partnership was crucial to the success of this project. In the first weeks a phone line to Chan's mother played a critical role. If Chan couldn't make herself understood and became distressed, which happened often at first, she went with a teacher to the office. The teacher would phone home so Chan could tell her mother the problem. Her mother would explain to the teacher in English so things could be resolved. This provided an instant translation service but also, crucially, reassured Chan so she could cope and carry on with the day.

Words relating to classroom topics were sent home on a daily basis, and translated and returned by Chan's mother, who supported the accelerated learning scheme for reading that the class teacher set up for Chan.

Dual language books

The school bought dual language storybooks from http://www.rdsbooks.com/ or http://www.mantralingua.com/ including stories already familiar to the other pupils such as *Not Now Bernard*, *The Very Hungry Caterpillar* and *The Enormous Turnip*, and encouraged Chan to read them in Mandarin and English.

Language support

It was important to provide visual clues and written dialogue cues. For example a visual timetable with pictures was made showing the activities that the pupils would be doing through the day. The relevant English words were included and Chan's mother translated the words and wrote the Mandarin equivalents alongside. These dual language words and phrases were collated into a *Dual Language Book* and shared with all the pupils. Providing this level of daily support helped Chan feel more secure

> I regularly translated English words for Chan and she was enthusiastic to get involved with this process. It made her feel important in the class to be given something to do. They asked me for simple phrases in Chinese to use in the class, like 'hello', 'enjoy your meal' and it made both of us feel valued.
> Chan's Mother

because she knew what was going to happen throughout the day. The school also made strong links with support staff from the Specialist Teaching Service and a member of this team came to school every week to help Chan develop her English.

Valuing the child's cultural background

The language resources to support Chan were shown to the other pupils so they could see another language. Each week Chan taught her classmates some expressions and phrases in Mandarin and each day the register was answered with a Mandarin Chinese greeting. The teacher built time into the school day for the class to talk about things Chan had done in China, and compared some elements of everyday life with Cumbria. The class used picture books about

> In her memory this first year was very important to her. That she was welcomed so much, she feels part of the community, she feels the UK isn't hostile to her. At home she had lots of English storybooks and a support teacher to help with reading. If the school hadn't done so much, she wouldn't feel so positive about coming to England. The main thing has been the feelings and environment at this school.
> Chan's mother

China (e.g. *C is for China* published by Oxfam). Chan talked about the activities she could remember from Chinese kindergarten and pupils made comparisons with their school.

The family in the local community

There are aspects to this situation which some of the staff in school hope to find the courage to address more directly. Although Chan's mother is married to a local man she admits that it is difficult for her to make friends in the community. Everyone is superficially friendly and there's no sense of hostility, but she feels isolated and not accepted into friendship groups. She thinks her accent is a problem but so are people's perceptions of China and Chinese people. She thinks there is a fixed image of China, which is that the British are more cultured and intelligent and that China is poor. She wants people to know that China is very diverse, but finds it hard to get this across. Teachers hope that when Chan's classmates grow up and are in a position to welcome people into their community they will be less prejudiced than their parents and grandparents.

Outcomes

The key to the success of this project lay in involving Chan's mother in ensuring that she was coping with her new language and environment, and also in increasing the Chinese cultural projects

the school undertook. This showed their only Chinese pupil how valued and welcome she was in school. It helped a pupil who spoke only Mandarin when she came in September to be able to contribute positively to the class throughout the year both in her own language and in English. The class now has one bilingual pupil and also many who can say basic phrases and greetings in a Chinese language.

Other activities

The Year 2 class uses a persona doll named Zelda, who has the persona of a child from a Travelling family. She is used to discuss incidents that may be happening between pupils in the class or in the playground. For example when there was a spate of kicking and nastiness, the teacher brought Zelda out and put a bandage on her leg. She said she was unhappy because there was kicking in the playground and she'd been hurt. Pupils were able to talk about the incidents and their playground behaviour improved.

Chinese culture week

As part of curriculum development, the school wanted to help pupils understand another culture so it was appropriate to choose China. With the catalyst of a Chinese artist and storyteller, Lip Lee, pupils were immersed in a Chinese culture week. Teachers felt that the involvement of two Chinese people, Lip

Lee and Chan's mother, with their diverse experiences, helped the celebration of cultural diversity to be authentic rather than tokenistic.

■ Lip Lee told traditional Chinese stories to give insight into the richness of oral story telling

■ Pupils learned songs in Cantonese

■ Pupils were taught the art of origami

■ Walls throughout school were decorated with Chinese lanterns, masks, lucky red envelopes and Chinese couplets

■ Pupils used nets to make Chinese red money bags. They learned about Chinese money and practised counting by putting specific numbers of coins into the red money bags.

The week culminated in a grand finale in the main hall with a parade of Chinese lanterns and a dragon dance. It was a magnificent occasion which involved all the children from nursery to Year 2.

Pupil taking part in the dragon dance.

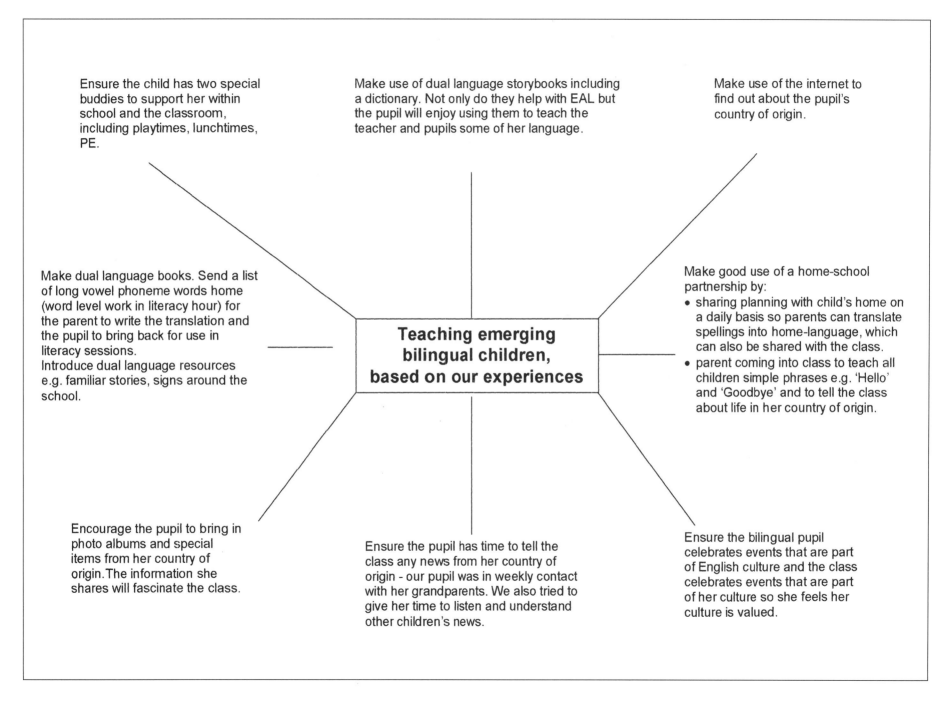

Ensure the child has two special buddies to support her within school and the classroom, including playtimes, lunchtimes, PE.

Make use of dual language storybooks including a dictionary. Not only do they help with EAL but the pupil will enjoy using them to teach the teacher and pupils some of her language.

Make use of the internet to find out about the pupil's country of origin.

Make dual language books. Send a list of long vowel phoneme words home (word level work in literacy hour) for the parent to write the translation and the pupil to bring back for use in literacy sessions.
Introduce dual language resources e.g. familiar stories, signs around the school.

Teaching emerging bilingual children, based on our experiences

Make good use of a home-school partnership by:
- sharing planning with child's home on a daily basis so parents can translate spellings into home-language, which can also be shared with the class.
- parent coming into class to teach all children simple phrases e.g. 'Hello' and 'Goodbye' and to tell the class about life in her country of origin.

Encourage the pupil to bring in photo albums and special items from her country of origin. The information she shares will fascinate the class.

Ensure the pupil has time to tell the class any news from her country of origin - our pupil was in weekly contact with her grandparents. We also tried to give her time to listen and understand other children's news.

Ensure the bilingual pupil celebrates events that are part of English culture and the class celebrates events that are part of her culture so she feels her culture is valued.

■ 3.4: Keeping Diversity on Track

The *Keeping Diversity on Track* project, devised by CDEC and funded by the government's Development Awareness Fund, involves five primary schools along the Carlisle – Settle railway line. The aim is to increase understanding of the richness and interdependence of the cultural diversity in the communities along the railway line. The objectives are to support the participating schools to:

■ explore and record the different contributions made by diverse groups and individuals to their school and local community life

■ increase understanding of the lives and communities of all involved by considering how these are affected by issues such as diversity, intolerance, inequality and unfairness

■ share local experiences and learn from those of others in different social or cultural communities

■ take responsibility for action to sustain community development or effect change in each community

During the first year this project is working with two urban schools from Carlisle (involving Year 5 and 6 pupils), two rural schools from farming communities in the Eden Valley (involving Reception, Year 1 and Year 2 pupils) and one school from a market town in the Eden Valley (involving Year 4 and 5 pupils).

Teachers from each school, led by CDEC, met and discussed the themes that could be used as a focus for exploring diversity within their communities. To help increase understanding of the range of groups in the community each school identified at least one local group to involve in the programme (for example the Women's Institute, Young Farmers, Age Concern, or church groups).

They agreed to incorporate into their project some of the values such as fairness, democracy and rights which underpin the eight Millennium Development Goals.

Two activity days were planned to enable joint exploration of each other's communities. The schools formed two groups: the first focused on journeys, leisure activities and learning disabilities, while the second group explored issues relating to employment.

Class-based work in all the schools began with activities that uncovered the perceptions already held by pupils about their own locality, and about the particular themes chosen for exploration.

All schools did the activity 'I live here and I think........' (see section 1.1).Variations on this activity were also used, such as:

'I hear the people who work here are...............................'	'I hear the people who work here come from..................';
'I like doing .... in my spare time.'	'My parents like doing.................. in their spare time.'
'The elderly people in the Thursday club like doing........................... in their spare time'	
'I think the children from there will think we are..................'	'I think the children from............... will be.....................'

Local audit

Pupils from each school gathered information about their locality through questionnaires to pupils, staff and parents and took photographs relevant to their chosen theme. They interviewed people in the community such as the elderly people's club, local food outlets, care homes and pupils' family members.

Joint Activity Days

Before and after the joint activity days each school undertook activities designed to uncover pupils' ideas of what their partner schools and localities might be like. The findings were recorded as concept maps.

During the activity days the pupils took part in joint art activities. One group of schools worked on a giant jigsaw puzzle representing diversity within and

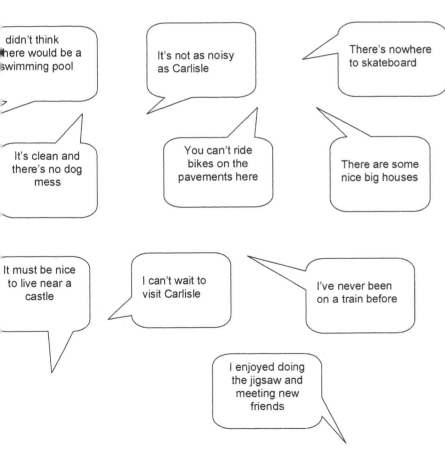

between their communities. The other group worked on a collage that depicted their perceptions and observations of their own and their partners' community and environment.

A total of 49 pupils aged 5-11, accompanied by teachers and parents from two of the schools, travelled from Carlisle and Penrith to meet their partner school further down the Settle-Carlisle line. On meeting, the pupils worked in pairs to find out three things about their partner and then introduced each other to someone else in the group.

Pupils from the host school shared the jigsaw pieces they had been working on and talked about which items had been chosen and why they were important. They included the river, the football ground, the castle, farms, swimming pool and hobbies. The pupils walked around the locality together to look for things that were the same and different to their own locality, things they found interesting and things they would like to have in their own locality.

During the afternoon all pupils worked on more jigsaw pieces, based on what the visiting pupils had seen during the walk. There was much discussion about what they saw and what they had expected.

Reflection and future plans

It was clear to all the adults that the pupils really enjoyed the experience of meeting one another. Some had expected the pupils from Carlisle to be 'rough and tough' but they changed their minds when they found how friendly they were. So prejudices about different localities within Cumbria were beginning to be challenged.

One teacher wondered how the Carlisle pupils would have reacted if they knew that some of the host pupils were from Gypsy/Traveller families. At this early stage of the project the class teachers were cautious and decided against deliberately introducing something. They wanted the pupils to get to know each other at their own pace. It is a longer-term objective of *Keeping Diversity on Track* to tackle such prejudices more directly by creating situations where the children, especially the Traveller pupils, feel comfortable to identify their heritage.

■ 3.5: Extending an overseas student's contribution across the school

The project took place in a rural primary school with 160 pupils on role. The school successfully applied to host a German student for two terms as part of the Comenius programme.

At a preparatory meeting the staff considered two key issues:

■ that this was a young woman who was visiting a strange country, so they wanted her to feel safe and happy in her new environment and

■ how she might enrich the school curriculum.

Staff wanted to ensure Gerda had a fulfilling experience and that the school would gain maximum benefit from the opportunity. It was suggested to Gerda that she bring certain items with her, such as familiar story books in German (for example *The Very Hungry Caterpillar*); a German teddy bear with

> The assistantship was supposed to be for five months but she stayed on an extra month at her own expense and we were really happy that she extended her stay. We would have liked her to stay all year!
>
> Headteacher

his suitcase full of items to help teach about life in Germany; and items for a German Christmas such as biscuit recipes.

Gerda spent three days each week in school, supporting teachers in the junior department during autumn term and the infant department during spring term. Once a week she also helped in the language department of a local secondary school and with a drama project alongside pupils from a special school.

Reception and Year 1

With this age group the aim was to help pupils understand experientially that there are other countries and other languages. Initially pupils would tell Gerda 'You speak funny'. By the end of the project they accepted her accent (and accents generally) and understood something about her background.

Gerda regularly added something from Germany into activity topics. For example, on the topic of birds she introduced a dance she remembered from her own school days; on the topic of magnetism, the pupils played a fishing game using magnets that came from Germany; and on the topic of houses she played a game that involved teaching some simple German words such as 'up', 'out', 'down'.

She first introduced the German-speaking teddy, Willi Bear, with groups of five or six pupils. The pupils slowly unpacked his suitcase and talked about the things they found inside: German money, passport, air ticket, a map of Germany, some pictures of his home town and his family. Gerda taught the pupils German for *Mum, Dad, please, hello*, etc which they much enjoyed. At Easter, Willi Bear brought chocolate eggs from Germany and hid them in the school garden for the children to find, and children painted eggs and hung them on the branches of trees in the German tradition.

Years 2, 3 and 4

These pupils had a general concept of other countries so Gerda aimed:

■ to show that it's real people who speak other languages

■ to develop the pupils' understanding of another country beyond the stereotypes of national dress, dances and traditions

■ to understand that places and people within a country such as Germany are very diverse

They learned that in many respects Germany isn't that different from England. For example by playing games and reading stories from Germany, they discovered that many were the same as some they knew in England.

Gerda's home of Essen was studied to fulfil the geography requirement of learning about another locality. Gerda set up a link with a primary school in Essen and acted as translator when the pupils emailed each other. The classes studied maps of each locality and asked lots of questions after watching videos and investigating photographs. They made a poster with pictures of themselves to send to their link school. Gerda developed the use of Willi Bear with this age group to make sure pupils didn't get a stereotyped view of German people, and when they celebrated a German Christmas she showed them that there are various ways that German people might celebrate the festival.

Years 5 and 6

Gerda helped pupils produce a video about their school to show to their link partners in Essen. Planning and timetabling for this was intensive and the project lasted several weeks. The pupils considered what might be the same in Germany and what might be different and included contrasting elements in their film. They were keen to address any stereotypes the German pupils might have about Britain. They also explored a geography topic on the Rhine and carried out independent work to produce a leaflet on their own chosen topic, such as *Legends of the Rhine; Wildlife around the Rhine;* and *Pollution of the Rhine.*

Outcomes

This project brought many benefits, largely because the experience of having an overseas student in the classroom was unique and exciting for the pupils. The school has decided to wait a few years before requesting a second student, so that the presence of an overseas student in school doesn't become commonplace and so lessen the excitement for pupils.

While this student was welcomed into the school and pupils responded well to her, some underlying stereotypes and perceptions of Germany did emerge. For example, one pupil told her she had heard someone say 'All Germans are like Hitler'. Gerda discussed this with the pupil and learned that the 'someone' was her father. Another said: 'My Grandad said the Germans bombed us, so why should we think well of them?'

An important learning outcome for staff was understanding that any visitor to school might expose stereotypes and prejudice, so the school needs to be vigilant, have procedures in place and be prepared to tackle the issues that arise in the curriculum. This applies not just to senior staff but to all adults in the school. With one-off day visits from artists, musicians or dancers it is too easy to focus on light-hearted topics and ignore or gloss over the tough issues of prejudice and negative attitudes towards people from other countries or cultures.

With someone who is there for a term there is greater incentive to expose the initial preconceptions which are the basis of prejudice and stereotypes.

The challenge of pupils bringing into school the prejudicial attitudes from their parents and grandparents is something that needs to be worked on. Teachers may not immediately equate racism with statements made against European cultures. This project showed how there are many opportunities to highlight and tackle attitudes towards Germany as a whole school, with an underlying challenge to wider prejudices and racism.

> *I really had an intensive experience with the children here. I was treated in a special way compared to other schools where they have an overseas student every year. I've learned more than all my time at university [training to be a primary teacher]. I came from a big city to this small village, so that was a shock. I did a lot of small group teaching and I saw how individual children work... and I saw how difficult it is to teach a language.*
>
> Reflections by the German student

■ 3.6: Supporting Traveller pupils in the classroom

Only 13% of respondents in the 2005 Cumbria Attitudes Survey said they knew someone who was a Gypsy/Traveller yet this is one of the largest ethnic minority groups in Cumbria. The finding confirms the low level of integration between the two communities. Given the evidence in relation to other minority groups, increased interaction between the settled community and the Gypsy/Traveller community may have the positive effect of breaking down barriers and reducing the relatively high negativity towards them amongst the general public.

In Cumbria, Romany Gypsies and Travellers tend to experience more hostility and racism than other groups. It

Scenes at Appleby Horse Fair

is estimated that only about 20% of Traveller children attend school, partly because of the misunderstandings and hostility they face. It is important to give all parents, children and staff the opportunity to discuss and support an equal access policy, explicitly including Romany Gypsies and Travellers. If children and their families can be helped to understand that everyone has a responsibility to welcome one another, prejudice against this group may begin to reduce.

This project took place in a primary school with over 200 pupils that has a long tradition of working successfully with pupils from travelling fairground families. The winter base for the fair is situated in the town and the pupils have a predictable travelling season, so they can be away for many months of the academic year.

The school has wholeheartedly embraced a range of opportunities to expand its practice in multicultural issues including race equality training and hosting the *Ally Comes to Cumbria* forum theatre production (see section 4.1). The Traveller education team within the Specialist Advisory Teaching Service (SATS) held an information-sharing workshop with school staff, where ideas were generated for more effectively supporting the Traveller pupils when they travel away from school. The school

agreed to be the pilot school for a distance learning strategy.

Distance learning is a scheme of independent learning that has been developed nationally, not as an alternative to school for Traveller pupils, but as a means to provide some continuity of education and equality of opportunity within a pattern of interrupted learning. It is a means of keeping children in contact with the school's curriculum and creating a sense of their belonging to the school community, while responding to and valuing their mobile lifestyle.

Through their designated teacher for Traveller pupils, the school is committed to working closely with SATS staff to ensure the distance learning is well planned, well resourced, evaluated and collaborative between school, parents, and pupils.

Six pupils were identified who were due to go travelling with their fair at Easter. The pupils were from a wide range of year groups: from nursery, reception, and Years 1, 2, 4 and 6. All the pupils and their parents were invited into the school. On the first occasion, they were given a tour of the school, met the staff and were given a presentation about the distance learning packs and how the system would work. All parents present agreed to be involved with the pilot and committed to support it. They agreed to provide the school with a list of sites and addresses that they would be visiting and when, as the fairground year is planned well in advance.

On a second visit the parents had informal discussions with staff and they collected the distance learning pack designed specifically for their child. These were made following assessments of the pupil's needs by both the school and SATS staff. Class teachers had provided work in three week blocks, focusing on basic skills in English, maths and science. This kept the task manageable for staff and realistic for pupils.

SATS provided the boxes for the distance learning packs, envelopes for returning the work, postcards, stamps, school address labels and an education contacts list (so parents could contact other Traveller education services around the country for support). Literacy and numeracy games, mini science projects and story tapes were provided to ensure the packs were diverse, stimulating and relevant to the curriculum.

The families provided photos of the children next to their stalls and rides for display on a school notice board, alongside a map of where the fair was going. Parents agreed to help their children keep in touch with their classmates via postcards. Communications from the travelling pupils were read out in their classes and displayed on the notice board and their classmates prepared greetings cards and letters for them. Completed work from the travelling children was all put on display and new work sent out. This worked well until the children returned in November.

The school is fortunate to have a member of the kitchen staff who is part of the Traveller community and regularly visits the fair on its travels. With the agreement of the other parents, she became the courier for work and other communication. Copies of school newsletters and letters were sent so the families could keep up to date with happenings at the school.

Outcomes

When the pupils returned to school after Bonfire Night they settled back into school very well. As they had moved up a year, their new teacher assessed the work they returned and implemented separate and appropriate integration support. All the communication with their classmates and the displaying of their whereabouts did a good deal for their status and made them feel that they belonged and were valued.

Travellers at Appleby Horse Fair

This pilot project has proved so successful that this distance learning strategy and supporting guidance documents will be developed for other schools in the county which have Traveller pupils, including pupils who have less predictable patterns of travelling than the fairground families.

■ 3.7: Including Traveller culture in the curriculum

The setting for this project was a primary school with over 300 pupils in a market town which hosts a large Gypsy Horse Fair annually. The school has embraced various opportunities offered by Cumbria Education Service to expand its practice in diversity issues, including race equality training, use of persona dolls and hosting antiracist forum theatre.

The headteacher was conscious that pupils absorb some of the local hostility towards the Gypsy community. Some residents are overtly negative about 'Gypsy Week' and the disruption it brings. Although some residents benefit from the business opportunities it brings to the town, other businesses make a point of closing during the week of the fair. During the build-up to the fair local schools finish early and bus routes are altered to accommodate the extra people, both Gypsies and tourists. So from an early age many children encounter a negative view of Gypsies and Travellers.

During the race equality training session staff discussed what they could do to promote a positive attitude towards the Gypsy community and expressed interest in exploring strategies. Some of them had never been to Fair Hill.

An advisory teacher worked with the KS2 co-ordinator to plan a Gypsy and Traveller awareness programme for the week before the annual fair for all classes, to help improve understanding of the culture and lifestyle of Gypsies and Travellers. The LEA organised an arts competition to celebrate the fair, and the school was keen to enter.

The aims
■ all classes to have the opportunity to consider and explore an aspect of Gypsy and Traveller culture and lifestyle

■ all staff to have the opportunity to familiarise themselves with appropriate curriculum materials to support on-going work

The intended outcomes
■ pupils would develop a more positive attitude towards Gypsies and Travellers

■ staff would consider how to include a Gypsy and Traveller perspective in the curriculum

■ a display would be made of work carried out throughout the school and art work entered for the competition

The criteria for success
■ pupils show positive attitudes towards Gypsies and Travellers in discussion

■ pupils show some knowledge and understanding of their lifestyle and culture

■ staff feel able to use the resources in future work

An invaluable resource used with all year groups was the set of four CDs of photos in the Gypsy and Traveller Picture Library: *Celebrating Diversity and Promoting Race Equality*, published by Durham and Darlington Education Service.

All work began by examining children's existing perceptions of Gypsies. This led to quality discussion and honest sharing, so much so that some of the work was left undone because it was more useful to give children time to ask questions and consider a range of answers.

When nursery and Reception pupils were first asked: 'I wonder what you know about Gypsies?' responses were generally:

These comments were discussed and generalisations were explored. Could they be true? Work continued in small groups. The advisory teacher used an Irish Traveller persona doll called Joe to tell his story and answer questions. Role play activities took place in the trailer home corner. Staff used photos of trailers, caravans and vardos to work on the pupils' attitudes, and answered questions about them.

When pupils in Years 1 and 2 were first asked 'I wonder what you've heard about Gypsies' their responses were similarly negative:

Gypsies are going to take me

They leave lots of litter

They are always fighting

These comments were discussed and stereotypes were explored. How would we know if they were true? Pupils were asked to sort the photos into categories of their choosing and to think of questions to ask about at least one photo. They enjoyed seeing their home town in the photos of the fair and were curious about what they saw. They also enjoyed the story book *A Horse for Joe* by Margaret Hird and Ann Whitwell, published by Wiltshire County Council.

When Year 3 and 4 pupils were initially asked 'What do you know about Gypsy Travellers?' responses were more positive. Some made comparisons with their own experience and lifestyle. Some children had been on holiday in a caravan or knew people who had. They discussed what it might be like to live in a trailer or vardo for much of the year and why Travellers may settle. When sorting the photos the pupils offered constructive comments and were interested in the lifestyle and culture depicted. They were motivated by the art competition, which was to design something which represented the fair, using any artistic medium.

In Years 5 and 6 some entrenched negative attitudes emerged when pupils were asked: 'What do you know about Gypsy Travellers?' The myth about Travellers never paying tax had to be dispelled. A balanced argument about

the issues appealed to pupils; the historical perspective was explained and they learned that 90% of traditional stopping places used for generations have recently been outlawed to Gypsies and Travellers. The range of views about Gypsies and Travellers was linked to literacy work on fact, opinion and rumour. Gradually some pupils recognised the contradictions in their opinions. They studied the photographs in detail and used them to ask many questions about Traveller lifestyle. They were interested in the arrangements for travelling children to keep up schooling. Were there any in their school, they wondered? They worked on plans to build a trailer and discussed how hard it would be to fit everything in.

As well as the resources already mentioned, pupils and staff had access to:

My Wonderful Place: the story of a journey to Appleby Fair by Sally Barter, published by London Borough of Hillingdon Traveller Education Service

A Time to Look Back: Appleby Fair over the last 50 years, published by Barrie Law

A Time to remember: A Collection of photographs of the travelling people and their way of life, published by Barrie Law

Outcomes

Given the entrenched nature of the prejudice against Gypsies and Travellers in the town, this work needs to be on-going. Teachers said they learned a lot from these sessions and feel more confident about incorporating some of the ideas into future curriculum planning. Some were inspired to visit Fair Hill. Many pupils realised how easy it is to take on board stereotypes of a whole community.

After the fair one boy said; 'I had never been up to Fair Hill. After we did the work in school about Gypsies I was really interested. I persuaded my parents and we went up there for the first time. We really enjoyed it'.

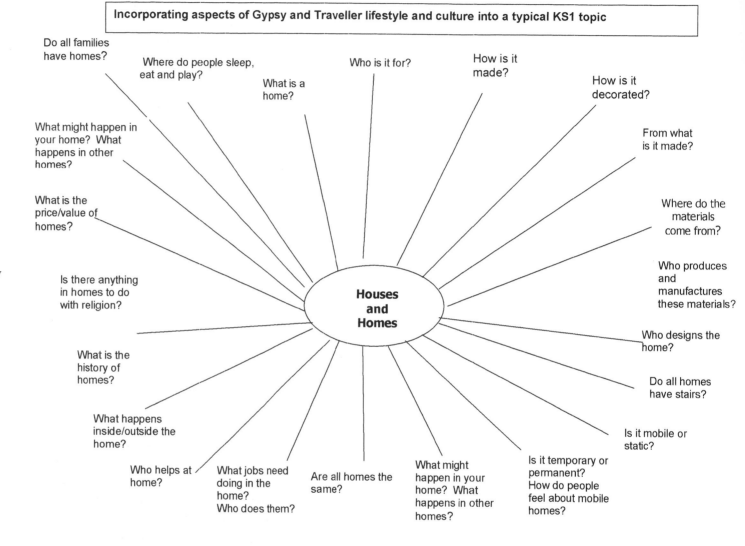

Incorporating aspects of Gypsy and Traveller lifestyle and culture into a typical KS1 topic

Houses and Homes

Do all families have homes?

Where do people sleep, eat and play?

What is a home?

Who is it for?

How is it made?

How is it decorated?

What might happen in your home? What happens in other homes?

From what is it made?

What is the price/value of homes?

Where do the materials come from?

Is there anything in homes to do with religion?

Who produces and manufactures these materials?

Who designs the home?

What is the history of homes?

Do all homes have stairs?

What happens inside/outside the home?

Is it mobile or static?

Who helps at home?

What jobs need doing in the home? Who does them?

Are all homes the same?

What might happen in your home? What happens in other homes?

Is it temporary or permanent? How do people feel about mobile homes?

■ 3.8: Responding to negative attitudes towards Islam

This took place in a rural village school, where the fewer than 50 pupils on role are taught in two mixed-age classes. The headteacher was aware of the growing Islamophobia in the media and worried that pupils had stereotypical views, associating all Muslims with terrorists. She invited an advisory teacher into school to work with the pupils.

The advisory teacher worked initially in the infant class, introducing the children to a persona doll with a Muslim background. The doll (Lamin) wanted to share his excitement about the birth of his sister and the ceremonies to celebrate it.

In the junior class of Years 3-6, pupils were asked, 'What do you think of when you hear the word 'Muslim'?' They were

given time to think, then in pairs they created a mind map to show their combined thinking, which was mostly very negative. Some of the comments were discussed and the meaning of words like 'generalisation' and 'stereotype' were made clear.

They were asked to draw what they thought a Muslim would look like. Many pupils drew men complete with beards and flowing robes. Yet when asked to draw a person from the nearest town (or to draw a Christian) there was much variety in the drawings. Some found it difficult to choose who to draw – child, adult, young, old. They were asked, 'which of you drew the 'right' person from the nearest town? Is there a 'right' when we are talking about a diverse group of people? So why did you find it easy to draw 'a Muslim'?' More discussion followed on the dangers of generalisation and stereotyping in either of the drawing tasks. Their drawings were kept to one side and later used to compare with what they drew in response to the same questions at the end of the activity.

From Google, the advisory teacher had downloaded images showing women, men and children of all ages from a variety of cultural backgrounds, dressed in different ways and doing different things.

Pupils were given a set of photographs and told, 'Here are some pictures of people who are all Muslim'. Years 3 and 4 were asked to work in groups of four to discuss and agree on at least five different ways of sorting the pictures. Years 5 and 6 were asked how many different ways they could sort the pictures, and whether they could decide on the most interesting category. The pupils found fascinating ways to sort the photos, according to age, whether groups or individuals, outside, or inside, men or women, modern, old fashioned, colourful or dull.

Many pupils were astonished at how diverse the Muslims in the pictures appeared to be, especially those who looked like 'western' women and men in business clothes. One child said: 'This can't be a Muslim. She looks like my mother'. Gradually pupils realised that anyone could be a Muslim, that they don't have to look a particular way and that not all hold the same views. After wide ranging discussion about the inappropriateness of judging from someone's appearance what their faith or culture may be, pupils were asked to fill in the following (see page 56).

Pupils were asked: 'Individually will those of you in Years 3 and 4 please choose the photo you like the best. Those of you in Years 5 and 6 please choose the photo that tells you most about the

a) Looking at the pictures, can you tell me 5 things about Muslims

1
2
3
4
5

b) I wonder if you can ask at least 5 questions about Muslims

1
2
3
4
5

c) Can you select your best question?

d) Choose one picture. can you give a title to the picture?

person in it. Notice all the thoughts you have whilst you are choosing. Once you have chosen, please explain to the others in your group why you chose that photo'. Then they discussed some of the following questions:

What five similarities do you think you have to this person? Why?

What five differences do you think you may have? Why?

If you met this person what would you like to know about them?

What do you think the person enjoys about life? Why?

What might the person's hope be for the future? Why?

Which of the people in these photos would you least like as a neighbour? Why?

Think of two questions you would ask them.

What do you think their answers would be?

Which of these would you least like as a friend? Why?

Which of these would you least like as a teacher? Why?

Which of these would you most like as a neighbour? Why?

Which of these would you most like as a friend? Why?

Which of these would you most like as a teacher? Why?

Outcomes
It was clear from what pupils had said that before this activity most had assumed all Muslims were alike. When they reflected on the activity, the pupils said: 'I didn't realise anyone could be a Muslim'; 'I was surprised how easy it is to generalise'; 'They aren't all the same'.

■ 3.9: Adapting antiracist education activities for pupils with special educational needs

This project took place in a school with over 50 pupils who all have severe learning difficulties. Although the pupils are adolescents and going through the angst and turmoil of that age, they are operating at a much lower level cognitively. So the issues they explore need to start from an appropriate point, one which might also suit mainstream primary pupils.

In geography the pupils were comparing two contrasting localities – the Lake District and Egypt. The starting point was a visit to Tarn Haws – in the rain. They noted the main features of the Lake District being quite beautiful and sometimes wet. They also saw photos of one of the teachers and her family with some Bedouins in the Egyptian desert.

Initially all the pupils thought that black-skinned people were from Africa and that there were none in the Lake District. They looked at pictures of people with different colour skin. The teacher has an olive complexion and the pupils noticed this. They said, 'They have dark skin like you'. A social worker who attends school is black, but pupils didn't mention this or make connections with her origins.

In a citizenship lesson, the book *The Skin I'm In* by Pat Thomas was used as the stimulus for a Philosophy for Children session. Pupils started by looking at the colour of people's hair and eyes and then talked about how they would feel if they were told not to do certain things because of their hair or eye colour. They were asked, 'What would it be like if only the fair-haired children could go out for playtime?' The pupils could relate well to this.

One of the questions in the book is: 'Have you ever been afraid of somebody that looked different to you?' This generated discussion about how some of the pupils feel when other people appear to be staring at them in the street. They explored the importance of getting to know a person before making judgements. From their own experiences, the pupils were able to identify with those who are bullied because of being

Fortress Europe publicity flier

from a minority group. This led into a lengthy discussion that enabled them to express their innermost thoughts about the way they are sometimes treated.

Refugees project

During a topic on World War II the pupils learned about refugees. They did role plays on saying goodbye to their parents. They had to think what they would take with them if they were told they had to leave home but could only take the few possessions they could carry themselves. There were some careful responses, including: 'I would take a picture of my family'; and 'I would take my teddy bears'. This contrasted with discussing what to pack to go on a holiday. As part of this topic they were invited to take part in the *Fortress Europe* exhibition (similar to, but simpler than, *Escape To Safety*, see section 4.2).

Outcomes

Philosophical enquiry works really well with pupils with special educational needs because of their honesty and their ability to empathise with each other. They develop their skills of listening, following-on and stating their opinion. They understand the rules and treat other members of the group with respect, listening to what they say and responding well to one another. They are able to explore curriculum topics or issues that have concerned them.

The pupils can empathise with others who have problems because they are constantly among pupils with severe difficulties. They always try to help their classmates join in with everything, so they can empathise strongly with children affected by war and how they might feel.

The teacher asked the pupils how they felt after experiencing *Fortress Europe*. Their responses were very empathetic: they talked about feeling scared and lonely. The teacher was able to impress on them what it must be like for people who have to leave their homes and families behind, sometimes at short notice. The exhibition was unlike anything they had experienced so made an impression on them.

Fortress Europe made me feel different to anything I have felt before

Afterwards they had a feedback discussion session with an advisory teacher which both staff and pupils found powerful. They had not talked about asylum seekers before, although there was much bad press about them. The concept of an asylum seeker was beyond the understanding of some of the students but they connected it with a 'country at war and having to get away for your own safety'.

Section 4
What teaching and learning strategies are effective?

Introduction
Every methodology described in this section can be a catalyst for high quality teaching and learning, and trigger insightful follow-up work. They should each be seen as part of a whole-school approach to be used across the whole curriculum.

Cumbria Education Service and CDEC have for many years promoted and supported the methodologies presented in this section. They reflect much of the multicultural and antiracist education taking place in Cumbrian schools.

Painting the trailer for Escape to Safety

■ 4.1: *Ally Comes to Cumbria* – an antiracist forum theatre production

Ally Comes to Cumbria is a specially commissioned piece of forum theatre for Cumbria's primary and secondary schools, produced by Global Link (www.globallink.org.uk) in conjunction with Cumbria Education Service. It tells the story of Ally, who arrives from Manchester to start at a new school in Cumbria. Ally is black and faces some adverse reactions from the pupils and teachers. A workshop following the performance gives pupils the opportunity to explore experientially how the characters could have acted differently.

Forum theatre is a participatory theatre method developed by the Brazilian dramatist Augosto Boal. It follows a basic structure where a central character fails to achieve a goal because of various obstacles. These obstacles are oppressions exercised by other people or power structures, which the audience have to try to overcome by finding solutions through the drama. During a second performance of the play the audience have the chance to step in and change the actions of a key character and so influence the outcome. For further information see www.cardboardcitizens. co.uk.

Cumbrian teachers are encouraged to use *Ally Comes to Cumbria* as part of a planned programme of preparation and follow-up work. The performance features racist incidents of name-calling, jokes, disrespect and bullying, both verbal and physical. It is realistic and powerful.

Teachers are advised to prepare pupils for the drama session with an activities pack and a video or DVD provided by Cumbria Education Service. These activities help pupils consider the terminology of race and challenge some of their own perceptions and stereotypes. They also help ensure the drama session is taken seriously and has the maximum impact in terms of raising awareness, challenging behaviour and fostering moral courage.

The drama
1. Pupils take part in a warm-up session using values-based drama activities, to begin clarifying their understanding of racism and preparing them to take part in the theatre workshop.

2. Pupils watch the performance, noting the prejudice and racism they see in it. The play, lasting about 25 minutes, is designed to show how prejudice can lead to serious racist incidents.

3. After the first performance the pupils are asked to work in pairs to think up situations when the character Cal (who tries to befriend Ally but is intimidated by a bully) could have acted differently to change the outcome. This helps the pupils talk through their ideas for changing the drama, ready for the second performance.

4. The four actors repeat the performance and pupils can put their hands up and stop the action when they want Cal to act differently. They are invited to intervene, either playing Cal's part or just explaining what Cal could do to change the outcome. This helps pupils to try out and evaluate a range of strategies for tackling prejudice and racism in a specific situation.

Ally Comes to Cumbria

An example of the dialogue in *Ally Comes to Cumbria*

ALLY   I thought Miss said you had to stay behind.

BILLY   Well she changed her mind, didn't she? She likes me. All the teachers like me. Not like you. You stink. You should go and live with the dirty Gippies – the Gyppos. You think you're going to be an actress one day? Ever seen a famous nigger actress? You're stupid, you. Come down from the jungle, hoo hoo, that's where you come from.

CAL   Come on.

   CAL pulls ALLY away.

BILLY   (*to CAL*) And you can get lost as well, you nigger-lover!

   BILLY exits.

ALLY   Thanks for getting rid of him. Everyone thinks he's so funny. He's like 'Ali G, respect'. He hates me. (Imitating Ali G) 'Is it cause I is black?'

CAL   It's just 'cause you're different. We've never had anyone coloured in the school before.

ALLY   I'd much prefer it if you said I was black.

CAL   Is that not rude?

ALLY   No. Everyone thinks it is, but it's not. Everywhere I go, people are looking at me. Whispering. Saying horrible things. It makes me wish I was white. It makes me wish I could just peel off my skin.

CAL   Hey it's not that bad. I'm sure they'll get used to you. Come on, it's English now. Come and sit by me.

Outcomes

The actors leading this drama find that in many schools some pupils, especially older boys, believe that physical aggression is an acceptable response to racist bullying. Schools are encouraged to plan a follow-up programme that explores a range of non-aggressive responses to harassment.

The following have arisen from the sessions as key issues that should be tackled in follow up work:

■ homophobia

■ issues around red hair

■ gender issues between boys and girls

■ the subtlety of stereotyping, for example words like 'Gypo' in the performance are rarely challenged by pupils

■ the difference between racism and stereotyping

■ that pupils often challenge bullying without seeing that it is racist

■ the culture of 'not grassing on your mates' which protects the bully

■ responses such as inappropriate laughing, for example laughing because the person next to you is laughing, or because Billy looks funny as a monkey

■ issues about why pupils focus on Billy (the bully) while Ally (the victim) gets ignored

■ issues about how comfortable the ethnic minority pupils may feel to make interventions

So far pupils from 162 Cumbrian primary and secondary schools have experienced *Ally Comes to Cumbria* and, increasingly, schools are booking it for the second time. Evaluations from Cumbrian schools describe some of the benefits of the experience for pupils:

> A fantastic experience for all the children. Sensitive issues were dealt with well. The characters were excellent and the children were able to relate to the whole thing. One child remarked afterwards that 'everyone should see the play on TV so they understand racism'.

This is a very good stimulus for further PSHE and citizenship work. From pupils' responses it was clear that they didn't realise that colour and culture could be discussed without being racist or offending anyone. One child said that 'black people could run fast because it was in their blood' – we have a lot of work to do on stereotypes!

A Year 6 pupil wrote:

> I am being very honest. I did used to sometimes say things. But I didn't realise what I was saying. After watching the play I really felt as if I was Black or Asian and I knew what it was to get picked on for my colour or religion. So I think that the play really helps you to know what a Black person might feel like.

Cumbria Education Service has commissioned a second piece of forum theatre called *Just Passing* which focuses on asylum seekers and Travellers. Schools are finding that it too is a powerful way of helping pupils and staff reflect deeply on racism.

■ 4.2: *Escape to Safety* – interactive exhibition on refugees

Escape to Safety is a multi-media, interactive, simulated experience of asylum-seeking, conceived and built by Global Link (http://www.globallink. org.uk/).

In its mobile 40-foot x 8-foot exhibition trailer, it is a sophisticated development of the successful *Fortress Europe* exhibition that was in huge demand and effectively used by Cumbrian schools. The exhibition has been hired by schools and community groups in Cumbria and also nationally, in an effort to respond to the rising prejudice and mistrust of immigrants and asylum seekers fuelled largely by the media. It aims to promote social justice and racial equality and challenge common perceptions of immigrants by giving participants a feeling of what it might be like to arrive in Britain as a refugee and seek asylum. Using experiential learning challenges the myths:

■ that asylum seekers are poor people in search of a more prosperous way of life

■ that asylum seekers are 'scroungers' who overwhelm our public services, and soak up our taxes by demanding benefits

■ that Britain is a 'soft touch' for asylum seekers, with its 'relaxed' asylum laws

Detention room in Escape to Safety.

■ that asylum seekers and refugees have nothing to offer to the British economy or culture

■ that most asylum seekers are criminals and some are terrorists

Escape to Safety takes participants on a multi-sensory journey through eight different rooms representing the stages on a refugee's journey to seek asylum in the UK. The trailer is parked at the host school or in the centre of a town for at least a week. Pupils experience it during the day and parents and members of the community are invited during evenings or weekends. When it is parked at secondary schools, feeder primary schools are invited to attend. Pupils, teachers, LEA staff and the public are given a taste of what it might feel like to be a refugee in Britain today. In most cases in Cumbria the host school has involved its local police education officer

in the project, and this has been an excellent opportunity to develop contact between the police, the school and the community – an important aspect of addressing racism.

To maximise learning and ensure ongoing work in schools, a project worker from a refugee background accompanies *Escape to Safety* and delivers teacher training and pupil workshops. These workshops aim to develop critical thinking skills, encouraging pupils to take a stand, and to assess and justify what they believe in. The activities help increase understanding and awareness of what causes people to leave, why refugees end up in a particular country, and what it might feel like to be in that situation. The role of the media is also analysed and questioned. Pupils are encouraged to suggest solutions to remedy xenophobic and racist attitudes in their schools and within the community.

Teachers find that the topic of asylum and migration is extremely relevant to citizenship, PSHE, English, geography, and history. For instance during Key Stage 2 pupils should be taught:

a) to talk and write about their opinions, and explain their views, on issues that affect themselves and society

b) to research, discuss and debate topical issues, problems and events

c) to reflect on spiritual, moral, social and cultural issues, empathising with other people's experiences

d) to think about the lives of people living in other places and times, and people with different values and customs

e) to realise the nature and consequences of racism, teasing, bullying and aggressive behaviour, and how to respond to them and ask for help

f) to recognise and challenge stereotypes

g) to realise that differences and similarities between people arise from factors which include cultural, ethnic, racial and religious diversity, gender and disability

h) to consider social and moral dilemmas they encounter in life, for example, encouraging respect and understanding between different ethnic groups and dealing with harassment

Outcomes

Evaluations of *Fortress Europe* and of *Escape to Safety* show that experiential arts-based learning of this kind, particularly when presented by a refugee, has effected attitudinal change in most of the pupils. In Cumbria it has also positively enhanced the relationship between schools and the police liaison workers who become involved when the exhibition is parked in the locality.

Evaluations strongly suggest that for the majority of pupils the experience is life changing. The results are striking when compared to the pupils' opinions prior to the exhibition. Responses to the words 'asylum seekers' and 'refugees' are normally elicited at the start of the workshop:

> They are scroungers; they steal our houses and money
>
> They are criminals and rapists
>
> They drive fast cars
>
> They have a life of luxury
>
> There are too many of them
>
> I don't like them because they smell
>
> They come here because they are poor
>
> They sneak into our country
>
> They are drug dealers and they bring guns into our country

By the end of the workshop, most pupils have a more informed idea about asylum seekers:

- 73% of those monitored stated correctly that asylum seekers are people escaping danger and persecution
- 65% disagreed with the notion that asylum seekers are 'bogus'
- 56% think that Britain does not have the highest percentage of asylum seekers and refugees in Europe
- 55% think that asylum seekers and refugees can make a great contribution to British society

The statistics show a move towards a more empathic behaviour towards asylum seekers:

- 77% stated that refugees and asylum seekers deserve our support
- 53% think we should give them more respect
- 49% think they need more help
- 41% felt ashamed of the way asylum seekers and refugees are treated in Britain

However:

- 21% still think asylum seekers should not be here;
- 23% think asylum seekers have nothing to offer to our society; and
- 11% think asylum seekers come here to look for an easy life and benefits

These results indicate that there is much to be done and still much misinformation that needs rectifying. Pupils who were interviewed a year after their experience of the exhibition had vivid memories of it and still remembered the main message: that refugees and asylum seekers are people looking for a safe place from which to rebuild their lives and that they should be treated with respect.

■ 4.3: Philosophical enquiry and Philosophy for Children

A Cumbrian primary school teacher who leads weekly sessions of Philosophy for Children in her classroom used *The Whisperer* by Nick Butterworth as a stimulus. One pupil said, 'The story isn't about cats is it? It's about black and white people. The black and white cats could represent black and white people. The ginger cats could represent Irish people because they sometimes have red hair. I know because I'm Irish.'

Many teachers and support staff feel it is taboo to talk about skin colour with young children. They say: 'Children don't notice', 'We don't want to draw attention to differences', 'Surely it is rude to talk about skin colour', 'I don't know what terminology to use'. However, we give mixed messages to children by not providing explicit opportunities to discuss differences. For example, allowing children to believe that it is rude to mention skin colour can lead them to believe that having a dark skin is somehow embarrassing or shameful.

Children are naturally curious about differences among themselves and others. Teachers need to respond to this interest and curiosity by providing them with a safe environment to discuss their thoughts, misconceptions, biases, stereotypes and prejudices. Philosophy for Children (P4C) allows children to talk openly and safely about difficult topics, including differences, the feelings associated with differences and to relate these to their personal experiences. With a picture book as stimulus, pupils can absorb and consider a range of cultural beliefs and expectations.

It is often possible to indicate through pictures things that are difficult to say in words. Good picture books deal with important human issues and convey complex ideas despite their economy of words. Children can learn about and question other cultures and other people's experiences through the visual narratives of picture books.

A Philosophy for Children (P4C) session

Philosophy sessions follow a common format. Pupils share a stimulus, usually a story – or a picture, object or activity – to generate philosophical questions. They choose a question to be the focus of enquiry, with the teacher guiding – not directing – the enquiry by asking questions that help pupils clarify, develop and build on each other's ideas. Philosophy for Children is described and discussed in many publications, in particular those produced by the Society for the Advancement of Philosophical Enquiry and Reflection in Education (see www.sapere.org.uk).

In a typical session as outlined on page 64 pupils talk about differences in an open and honest way. They quickly move from reflecting on the story and the question, to their own experiences.

Pupils interact in the dialogue at their own level, which ranges from quite complex dialogue to acknowledgment of personal attributes. In that session the pupils were particularly struck by the fact that some family members had similar features whereas others did not.

After the P4C session the pupils were visited by a genetics scientist who explained why people are all different, indeed unique, and introduced the concept of genes. This extended the philosophy work and also added to the science topic on Ourselves in which pupils explored differences.

ANY QUESTIONS?

WHERE DOES PREJUDICE COME FROM?

IS MEDIA INVOLVEMENT GOOD OR HARMFUL?

WILL YOUNG PEOPLE BE LESS RACIST THAN THEIR PARENTS?

WHY DO PEOPLE FOCUS ON DIFFERENCES?

IF WE DIDN'T KNOW ABOUT RACISM WOULD WE INVENT IT?

HOW CAN WE RECOGNISE A RACIST?

ARE THERE PLACES IN BRITAIN WHERE RACISM DOESN'T EXIST?

IS RACISM A CULTURAL CONCEPT?

WHOSE PROBLEM IS RACISM?

DO WE NEED PREJUDICE?

IS IT DELUDING OURSELVES TO DISMISS RACISTS AS SMALL-MINDED; AREN'T THEY CLEVER, MANIPULATIVE AND DANGEROUS?

DIVERSITY AND INCLUSION CONFERENCE JULY 2003

QUESTIONS RAISED IN P4C WORKSHOP BY TEACHER DELEGATES

That's My Mum by Henriette Barkow published by Mantra

That's My Mum is a picture book about two friends who have dual heritage. The book was read as a stimulus for two one-hour Philosophy for Children sessions with a Year 2/3 class. The story was broken down into three distinct sections that provided an opportunity to explore the different aspects of the story.

Introducing the Stimulus **Session 1**	Pupils' responses
1) Read first two pages and give individual and paired thinking time. Feed back to the group.	Children's initial reaction was disbelief: 'That can't be her Mum, they are different colours' and 'You can't have a white Mum if you are brown'. One child remarked that a child in school was brown yet his Mum was white. This led to children giving many reasons and examples of dual heritage families they had seen.
2) Continue reading story until the section where the two friends are thinking of ideas to help other people understand whose Mum is who. Give individual and paired thinking time to generate ideas for how they can solve the dilemma, and then record ideas on a flip chart. Encourage children to decide whether the ideas would be effective and what other aspects should be considered, giving reasons to support their arguments.	A range of ideas were offered, from wearing masks or sunbathing, to the Mum explaining to the rest of the children. There seemed to be two distinct ideas emerging; the child changing his/her appearance to look more like the Mum; and a more explanatory approach. The latter idea was more favoured as the discussion progressed.
3) Read the rest of the story. Give paired thinking time leading to the generation of philosophical questions. Pupils write these questions on a large sheet of paper to be displayed in the class during the week.	Philosophical questions generated by children: *Why did they want to change? Why was the boy's Mum brown?* *How do people not know which Mum is which?* *How did she turn brown? Why did they make fun of her?* *Were they really their Mums? Why was the boy's Mum white?* *What was the matter with the people that made fun?*
Session 2 4) Children to look at a variety of photographs of dual heritage families from magazines and teaching packs on families. Paired thinking time. Recap on story and questions.	Photographs were shown in response to the question 'Were they really their Mums?' There seemed to be some discussion on whether the story could be true because it was a picture book!
5) Democratic vote for one question using omni-vote technique	Chosen question: 'Why do people not know which Mum was which?'
6) Philosophical dialogue with the facilitator intervening where appropriate	Wide-ranging dialogue and pupils very engaged and involved.
7) Ending the enquiry	Many children contributed to the final review

SEATED IN A CIRCLE, SHARE A STIMULUS
This might be a book, a story, a poem, a video, an information text, a non-narrative text, a picture, a sculpture, an artefact

THINKING TIME
- Each pupil sits quietly for a few moments, jotting down the thoughts or concepts that come to mind and their own questions
- In pairs pupils discuss the issues that interest them, develop philosophical questions and decide on one only to present to the group, or
- Each pair collaborates with another pair to agree on one question, which is then written up on large paper with their initials

CATEGORISE THE QUESTIONS (Optional if there is time)
Invite pupils to make links between the questions, asking whether some are the same or similar, if one is part of another, and use different coloured pens to indicate these links

ENDING THE ENQUIRY: Select one:
- Ask for final thoughts on the question
- Summarise the key concepts discussed, for example by asking who can remember some of the ideas that have emerged
- Allow thinking time, then ask if anyone wants to say how their thinking may have changed as a result of the discussion, or if anyone has any thoughts on 'thinking about thinking'
- Vote yes, no or not sure about whether their thinking has changed as a result of the enquiry

AIR THE QUESTIONS: Select one:
- If someone is not sure about a question they can ask for clarification.
- Each pair talks to the group for 1 minute about their question
- Each pair talks about all the questions for 1 minute

FACILITATE DISCUSSION BETWEEN THE PUPILS
This is done through teacher silence, encouraging body language and facilitative questions to help the thinking of individuals and the group
The teacher is a facilitator who encourages collaboration and quality thinking

BEGIN THE ENQUIRY
The pair who originally formulated the chosen question express their first thoughts on it. Before opening the discussion to the whole group pupils can discuss it in pairs for two minutes, or write down their first impressions for one minute

VOTE DEMOCRATICALLY: Select one:
- Omni-vote - pupils vote for as many questions as they want to (easier to get a majority)
- Multi-vote - pupils have 3 votes each to use on 3 questions or 3 votes on one question
- Single vote with eyes shut
- Voting with a reason e.g. I like question 2 and will vote for it because....

■ 4.4: Building on philosophical enquiry to tackle antiracist education

This school had identified a need to tackle antiracist and multicultural issues and set aside a full day for the mixed Year 1/2 class to begin this programme. The morning session was described in section 1.7. The afternoon session built on the issues raised during the morning activity and introduced philosophical enquiry, which was new to these pupils.

Pupils were introduced to Philosophy for Children by watching a section of the BBC Transformers *Philosophy for Six Year Olds* video (available from SAPERE) that shows American school pupils taking part in a philosophical enquiry into what makes a person real. This stimulated the class into discussion and pupils concluded that people can share things such as where they live, language, colour of eyes and skin, but people are not the same. The class enjoyed seeing other children of their own age on the video and commented: 'it helped me think about what I was doing'; 'it helped me because I'd not heard of philosophy before'; 'it was interesting listening to them talking about things we'd not heard about'; 'it made me think a lot'.

The structure and protocol of a typical Philosophy for Children session were explained. The advisory teacher said she would read part of a story and that the pupils were to think about big questions, just as the children in the video had done. A big book version of *Something Else* by Kathryn Cave and Chris Riddell was used and smaller copies of the book were shared in twos and threes. This book has been used successfully in many Cumbrian schools as a stimulus to open up discussion on issues such as prejudice, bullying, racism, loneliness and self-esteem.

The advisory teacher read to the point in the story on page nine where the animals say: 'You don't belong here' ... 'You're not like us. You're Something Else'.

In individual thinking time pupils were asked to consider words which described their thoughts and feelings about the story so far. They shared some of these words with the person sitting next to them, then as a whole group. Pupils affirmed and challenged each other's words and phrases which the advisory teacher recorded on the board. They included:

Selfish; naughty; nasty; rude; lonely; out numbered; heart broken; respect; pathetic; not like us; no friends.

In pairs pupils were instructed to think of a question that they would like to ask of any of the characters in the book. Some of their questions were as follows:

- ■ *Who made you lonely?* (2)
- ■ *Why are you being pathetic to me?* (7)
- ■ *Why don't you like me?* (7)
- ■ *When are you lonely?* (8)
- ■ *Why can't you play with me?* (9)
- ■ *Why are you mean to me?* (13)
- ■ *Are you really lonely?* (22)
- ■ *What are you?* (30)
- ■ *Why aren't you playing with me?* (31)
- ■ *Why aren't you respecting him?* (37)

The advisory teacher asked if any of the questions were similar, for example those on the theme of 'loneliness'. She congratulated pupils on the number of 'why' questions, as these are open and encourage the search for a range of reasons rather than one easy answer. She explained that there were no right or wrong answers and that changing your mind about your original opinion is a very acceptable thing to do.

Pupils used an omni-vote process to determine which question they would most like to discuss and try to answer. This voting system gives pupils the freedom to vote as often as they want, using a show of hands. No hands means they don't want to discuss it; one hand means they would like to discuss it; and two hands means they really want to discuss it. The number beside each question indicates the number of votes.

The chosen question 'Why aren't you not respecting him?' got to the heart of the story and provoked serious discussion. The pupils started by trying to define the word 'respect'. They understood that being 'pathetic' to someone because they were different was wrong, yet thought some people were disliked because of how they looked. They shared ideas about not being liked and not being the same and concluded that it is important to give someone a chance and not judge people just on how they look or behave. Not everyone contributed but all were focused on listening to each other to develop their opinions. This methodology created a safe environment in which to express views on difference and helped promote an atmosphere of respect for other people's feelings.

Some of the Year 2 pupils were asked what they thought philosophy was, based on their work with *Something Else*. They said:

- *combining ideas together to make me think*
- *it's a way of getting more ideas into my head so I can think*
- *thinking harder*
- *thinking is easier because we are sharing ideas*
- *thinking about what people are like, what they do and why they do it*
- *asking questions to try to understand*

Follow-up activities
Thought bubbles

In a later session the class teacher gave pupils a photocopy of the illustration at the point in the story where the animals are saying: 'You don't belong here. You're not like us. You're something else'. A thought bubble had been added and pupils were given time to think how Something Else might be feeling. They used the space at the bottom of the sheet to jot down their ideas before writing in the thought bubble what they thought might be going through his mind as he walked away. Some Year 1 pupils needed adult support to scribe their ideas.

The class teacher asked the Year 2 pupils to use colours to show how each character might be feeling. They chose colours and outlined each character in the illustration to translate the range of feelings into colours. They designed a key to the colours, a method of recording their empathy which appealed to visual and kinaesthetic learners.

When the class gathered, each pupil shared their thought bubble with the group, many very expressively. The Year 2 pupils could also explain and justify their choice of colours. Two pupils were selected to go in turn into the hot seat as Something Else and pupils questioned the character in role. Many asked about being lonely and why Something Else wanted to stay at home. The following

dialogue ensued (B was child in role as Something Else):

A – *Why are you just going to walk away?*

B – *Because it's just part of life, I'm just going to have to accept it.*

C – *Why do you have to accept it?*

B – *You tell me, what can I do? I'm small and no one will help me.*

D – *Why should you be unhappy and lonely? They're just being mean.*

E – *They're not bothered about you – they're happy together.*

B – *They've seen others like them before but they haven't seen a stranger like me.*

F – *I sort of agree, they've seen others doing things like them and not the way you do it.*

C – *Why don't they notice they are all different... different to each other?*

The final comment provoked careful examination of the illustration in a follow-up session and the pupils discussed the idea that not all the animals were equally hostile to Something Else. Pupils noticed that one of the rabbits had its ears down and its body language may indicate that it was not as hostile to Something Else as the other animals. The teacher introduced the idea of peer group pressure and asked why they thought the rabbit hadn't done something to stop the hostility and befriend Something Else. Pupils discussed the difficulties of feeling out-numbered and being so scared, unsure and worried by friends' expectations that we will go along with their reactions.

Pupils did a further activity using a thought bubble, but this time relating to the range of animals rather than to Something Else. They wrote what some of the other creatures might be thinking, indicating a diversity of views from complete rejection to feeling sorry at his treatment and wanting to include him. Their responses showed they understood how easy it is to hurt someone just with words.

Conscience Alley

The class was divided into two groups: Rabbits and Other Animals. They formed two parallel lines. Pupils took it in turns to be Something Else. The Other Animals had to think about one of the comments they had written into their thought bubbles, then repeat it over and over again as Something Else passed by. The Rabbits had to think what they would say to Something Else if they had the courage.

The power of this medium is reflected in what pupils said about being Something Else:

> *'I felt sad because they were saying words they aren't meant to say'*
>
> *'I felt depressed and scared because I couldn't fight back'*
>
> *'The rabbits made me feel a bit happier'*
>
> *'I felt outnumbered and heartbroken'*
>
> *'I felt like I didn't belong'*

The pupils said this experience helped them to understand what it might be like to be Something Else. It made them stop and think, and the teacher hopes that the learning will have an effect on their behaviour both in and out of the classroom.

Outcomes

The class teacher used Philosophy for Children again, using the story *Beegu* by Alexis Deacon as the stimuli. This is about a small alien accidentally left behind on earth and how she is received by humans. The class voted to enquire into the question '*Why is she alone?*' and this led to an analysis of the difference between being alone and being lonely. Pupils agreed that Beegu was behaving strangely because things were so different to where she comes from. The discussion focused on how people were reacting towards her because of her appearance, and the pupils thought about how they would have reacted to Beegu.

The teacher experienced one of the most moving moments in her teaching career during this philosophy session. When one of the pupils had first joined the class from Pakistan, speaking no English, a classmate had asked 'Is he a terrorist?' This wasn't an aggressive accusation but a genuine enquiry based on his poor understanding of news events. The remark stemmed from his anxiety about world events and it is an example of the power of the media to influence a child's views. There is a real possibility that this, unchecked, could lead to racist beliefs.

During the enquiry the pupil who had come to Cumbria from Pakistan said: 'I know exactly how Beegu feels. I've felt like that. But I've found friends and people who like me now'. The pupils fell silent for a while then his classmate said: 'He has been very brave. I've never thought about how hard it had been for him', and all the pupils spontaneously applauded.

Philosophical enquiry can help pupils increase their understanding of the diverse world around them. Part of valuing this diversity is allowing children to confront their negative emotions about difference and teaching them skills to transform those negativities. Philosophy for Children is one way of developing these skills in a challenging but non-threatening way.

The class teacher was interested in the range of vocabulary choices, the intensity of emotions expressed about attitudes to difference, the deep empathy with Something Else and Beegu, the ability of some of these young children to understand that life isn't simple and emotions can be very complex, and the growing awareness of how we show feelings and reactions in non-verbal ways, for example through body language.

When asked at the end of the school year to reflect on what they had most enjoyed, many pupils said it was the philosophy sessions. As one pupil said, 'I like the talking. It got my ideas in my head'. And this time Ofsted commented on the unusual ability these young children showed to explore complex issues in depth.

■ 4.5: An enquiry approach at Foundation Stage

The setting was a nursery school with over 100 children which has a long-standing commitment to promoting and developing enquiry skills in very young children. The headteacher had taken part in the *Making Sense of my World* project led by CDEC and Cumbria Early Years Partnership, which explored how to bring an enquiry approach into teaching *Knowledge and Understanding of the World* at Foundation Stage.

The project showed how a move towards child-led experiences and enquiry can help develop learning and thinking skills in a profound way. Based on children's unusual questions and observations in everyday situations, it looked at how adults could best respond then and there.

Young children need stimulus to encourage them to enquire about the world so the learning environment is crucial. Once children have the space to ask questions and make observations, these need to be followed up, not dashed, by the adult. The stimulus might be their curiosity about an object, idea or activity. It could be planned by the teacher, or related to something the child has brought into the setting. The adult response is the crucial factor in nurturing an enquiry approach in Foundation Stage settings.

One of the nursery class teachers attended a Philosophy for Children training course with a view to introducing enquiry in the nursery setting. She recognised that the standard format for Philosophy for Children needs adaptation for nursery settings.

This teacher introduced enquiry session twice a week with five or six pupils at a time, so it took some weeks to involve the whole class. The first session with the whole class used a picture from the book *I Wish I Didn't Have To Sleep* by Keith Hamel. The teacher opened the enquiry by asking what they thought about the picture, eliciting responses such as: 'there are aliens inside it'; and 'the pink one is a girl'.

The teacher had noticed that the children were displaying gender stereotypes in everyday play settings, playing with toy figures according to the perceived roles of men and women as, for instance, police or nurses. They reinforced their ideas about gender in various ways, for example: 'this must be a girl because it has brown hair'. The teacher started challenging such thinking by picking up on casual comments and suggesting they look around the class. She asked 'is everyone with brown hair a girl?'

For the second session the teacher used a large picture called *Birthday Party* (Nelson Thornes 2001, Stepping Stones, Unit 1 Week 1, Birthday Party, Ourselves). Initially she only revealed the part of the picture showing the dog. Children were asked for their ideas about what else there might be in the whole picture. More was gradually revealed (the food on the table) and then more (some of the presents) and finally the whole picture.

At each stage the children talked about what they thought was happening in the picture. When they could see it all, discussion focused on the child on the left of the picture with a blue jumper and long hair. This challenged their expected view of gender roles and aroused much disagreement over whether this was a boy or a girl. This process enabled the children to use their imagination and practice skills of deduction and reasoning, and justify their reasoning when others disagreed. They remained engaged on the activity for ten minutes – a long time for 3 and 4 year olds.

A third session used photographs of children in different situations, chosen to challenge gender and race stereotypes. The photographs were shown one at a time and the group were asked 'What are they doing?', 'Do girls or boys do that?', 'Who would be your friend?' and so on.

'Girls have long hair' [child]; 'Do they always?' [adult]; 'Yes they could do' [child]

'That's boys' things' [girl]; 'What things?' [adult]; 'But I like them too, like quad bikes' [girl]; 'So if you like them maybe they are girls' things?' [adult]

Outcomes

The staff have tried to reflect ethnic diversity in their purchasing, by buying black dolls and toy figures for small world play from a range of backgrounds. The class teacher became aware of occasions when racist language was used. When a child used the word 'nigger' it was clear that he didn't understand what he had said but had picked it up from an adult.

This project started to develop the ability of the 3 and 4 year olds to listen to others and helped them begin to see they could change their own views accordingly. The pupils said they could now listen to one another's ideas. The teacher plans to continue this methodology to explore the pupils' ideas on difference by using *Elmer* by David McKee, a story about a colourful patchwork elephant who tries to make himself the same as the other elephants.

Any enquiry activity with children this young will be short and may not appear to offer profound insights or deep understanding. But the skills being nurtured will be vital in developing these children into critical thinkers as their learning develops.

■ 4.6: An overview of school linking

School linking in Cumbria

Many schools in Cumbria are actively involved in a school link or looking for a linking partner. Some are linking with countries outside Europe as a strategy for teaching multicultural education and the global dimension, others are linking within the UK, some of them within Cumbria, in an effort to broaden pupils' horizons and tackle issues of diversity closer to home.

Several of the activities described elsewhere in this book include an element of school linking. For example, activities to challenge perceptions (see section 1.2 and 1.7) and linking within the UK (see section 2.3, 3.4 and 4.7). Other projects in Cumbria include:

■ a secondary school link with Tanzania that includes a group of primary schools in the Penrith and Carlisle area, working towards curriculum development

■ a cluster of schools on Walney Island linking with the Seychelles to study energy use and climate change

■ a nursery school in Whitehaven linking with a rural nursery school a few miles away, to tackle some of the prejudice that exists between towns and villages in West Cumbria

---

Criteria of good practice for school links

A link is an equal partnership, signified by:

■ a jointly conceived and regularly reviewed partnership agreement

■ a rolling programme of planning and review, undertaken jointly by to ensure the link continues to meet the needs of both schools

■ shared curriculum projects undertaken as an integral part of the link

There is whole-school involvement, for example:

■ the link is embedded in the school development plan

■ the link has a significant curriculum development dimension involving a range of curriculum areas and subjects

■ the link is supported by, and involves, adults from across the school including non-teaching staff, parents and senior management

Other aspects of the link should ensure:

■ having structures in place for its future development

■ that the schools continue to consider their motivations in having a link and the implications of these for their partner

■ that fundraising within the context of the link is carefully considered and not taken for granted

■ that the schools understand the pitfalls of linking and recognise the implications of the long-term nature of their commitment to a link.

from CDEC's School Linking and Global Citizenship Programme

■ a rural primary school in the Lake District National Park, linking with an urban school in Barrow

■ a cluster of schools in the Eden Valley, linking with Tower Hamlets to introduce multicultural diversity issues

■ two secondary schools in Cumbria linking with schools in Mexico City, using philosophical enquiry to help the pupils learn about shared citizenship issues and to provide a focus for communication and exchange visits

...link can contribute significantly ...obal citizenship education across ...he whole school. However there are many challenges inherent in linking, and the goals of global citizenship will not be achieved *just* because a school has a link. Without careful management, a link is just as likely to confirm stereotypes of other people and places, and of development issues, than to challenge and change them. This means that the school must work hard to build in activities that openly discuss and explore the perceptions of other places held by pupils (and staff), and to revisit these regularly. A link which focuses largely on fundraising for development projects or child sponsorship will only reinforce stereotypical views of rich and poor, and will not be tackling goals of global citizenship. For the aims of global citizenship see www.oxfam.org.uk/coolplanet.

Learning points from Cumbrian experiences of school linking
It can take two years for a link to be properly established
Linking takes time. It requires negotiation, learning to communicate, shared planning and serious commitment by both partners. It is not a coincidence that the ones that have flourished are those reporting a strong personal and working relationship between the partner teachers.

Incorporating the link into existing plans
When incorporating the link into curriculum plans, it works better to build on activities that are planned already. Constant communication between partners is essential. Holiday, exam and other key dates and commitments must be shared so that timescales can be agreed that are realistic to both schools.

Commitment
Linking isn't an easy activity that can be delivered off the shelf. A high level of commitment is needed by a range of staff in the school to establish a link and build it into curriculum plans, whether in one class or across the school.

Communication
Don't expect communication to be easy and smooth: it won't be. Even where both partners have access to email, communication isn't just about sending messages. It is about understanding and sharing the link objectives, coping when one partner is overwhelmed with other commitments, having strategies for when there are staff changes, and so on.

Partnership agreement
Communication problems will destroy a link if there isn't a shared partnership agreement with agreed aims and objectives. Do not have a link without it! It is all-important and takes time to work out. The link must have shared aims and each partner must get what they need

from it. Ask yourself why the partner school might want to link with you? If your partner's ideas and curriculum are very different, what will you do? Look for common interests, topics and ideas that you can plan together, and be specific. The link may not be high on the priority list for the partner and this can impact on what *you* expect.

Fundraising
You are likely to be asked for financial support and fund-raising at some time in your link, so think this through. How will you handle this when it comes up? If the link turns into a financial relationship (sponsoring children, for example) then it will not be an equal relationship, you may be reinforcing stereotypes and the goals of global citizenship may not be met.

Tackling perceptions through linking
Teachers need to start by looking at the current perceptions held by pupils, as they can not be tackled if we don't know what they are. This is vital, but is also very challenging, because the perceptions of the adults also need to be identified. One teacher's attitudes can influence everyone's learning. Examples of activities designed to identify perceptions are described in section 1.

The perceptions of the UK held by overseas partners can be enlightening. For example, when Mexican secondary school pupils were asked to give their views of the UK as part of their link with Cumbria they said: 'It is a very good country'; 'There are lots of people who are intelligent so it is very developed'; and 'They are mentally and physically better than us'. If their view of us can be so incomplete and inaccurate, what does it say about our view of them?

Pupils can be asked to put together a photo-and-artefact set that represents their village or town, or that represents Cumbria or even England. They will find this difficult, because of the diversity of lifestyles, interests and backgrounds, even among neighbours. And this will help them understand that they can't easily get to know another place just by seeing some photographs or artefacts.

Schools must consider how their link moves on from cultural celebration to tackling some of the underlying issues and messages of global citizenship education.

■ 4.7: School linking visits within the local community
Making banners: an arts project to challenge rural and urban perceptions in Cumbria

This project involved pupils in Years 3 and 4 from an urban school with 120 pupils in an area of high socio-economic deprivation, and pupils in Years 3, 4, 5 and 6 from a school in a rural environment with 60 pupils on role, drawn from a range of socio-economic backgrounds.

This link was set up by CDEC and the National Trust. It aimed to bring together contrasting schools onto a National Trust property to work on a joint piece of art work, and reflect their shared sense of place. A National Trust facilitator and two artists worked with the pupils at various stages of the project to design and make three banners which depicted the features of the different localities. The first two banners related to the schools' own environments and the aspects pupils identified with in their own locality. The third banner related to the environment around Acorn Bank, the National Trust property, and the pupils' perceptions of Acorn Bank in relation to their own schools and locality.

As described in section 1.2, the link initially involved the two schools finding out about their own environments through a local audit. After a walk to explore the local environment and identify elements the pupils considered important, the top twelve elements were recorded with photos and sound recordings.

Pupils identified their perceptions of the other school's environment, and then the photos and audiotapes were exchanged and compared. As part of identifying similarities and differences between the two localities, the schools used the photos and tapes as the stimulus for a philosophical enquiry to consider the preconceptions they had about each other's schools.

Designing the banners together gave a context for the pupils to express their ideas and feelings about their locality and reflect their shared sense of place. The identified similarities and differences were incorporated into the banner designs, creating opportunities to question and explore their perceptions of each other's places.

The second meeting was at Acorn Bank, a National Trust property. The pupils were sharply aware that they were meeting children from somewhere different. It took time and some icebreaker team-building games before they could work happily together and develop friendships. Two artists worked with the pupils and staff to make the banners depicting their own localities.

During their third meeting, again at Acorn Bank, the pupils explored the site and identified similarities and differences between their environments and that of Acorn Bank. These ideas formed the basis for the third and central banner and this was designed by working cooperatively. When hung together, the banners were linked by a central theme, a river which unites the three different localities. The banner-making sessions, with their interaction, fun and cooperative learning in an unconventional setting, were greatly enjoyed.

The schools came together for a fourth time to celebrate the banners. The press were present to record the activities, which included games and a shared picnic to foster the pupils' new friendships. The completed banners were displayed at the Cumberland Building Society in Carlisle, then returned to the schools.

Outcomes

This project provided a positive experience for the pupils in both schools. They began to learn about other parts of Cumbria and some remarked that having no language barrier made communication easier. The link allowed pupils from the urban school to experience the beautiful rural setting of Acorn Bank.

The banners

By working with artists and children from different backgrounds, pupils developed a range of skills together. The fact that both schools were in Cumbria made it practical for them to meet and work together. Most importantly, children met pupils from the link school, whom they now refer to as 'our new friends'.

■ 4.8 Persona dolls

Originally created by Kay Taus, persona dolls represent all kinds of people from every background and ethnicity, as relevant to each context. Each is given its own name, age, personality, home, family and cultural background, likes, dislikes and friendships. The dolls are used to tell stories that raise equality issues. This is a powerful and enjoyable way of helping young children unlearn existing stereotypical views (see *Combating Discrimination: Persona Dolls in action* by Babette Brown, Trentham 2001).

As persona dolls belong to the adult, not the children, they are treated differently from other dolls. They don't live in the home corner. It is important that the doll comes to visit. Any doll can be a persona doll but child-size soft-bodied dolls are preferred. Persona dolls are not puppets so the teacher doesn't speak as if he/she were the doll. Instead the teacher listens to the doll and tells the pupils what the doll says, asking open-ended questions to the class such as, 'What would you do if....?', 'She says it makes her feel sad, do you ever feel...?', 'What do you think...?', or 'Can you help...?'

The idea is to introduce a doll and use it to tell stories about the doll's life as a way of exploring experiences. Stories are woven around the doll for the rest of the year. It is best to start with happy stories and a male doll to counter any prejudice

Three persona dolls donated by Cumbria Education Service and available for loan from CDEC

from boys against dolls. The aim is to develop pupils' ability to empathise with the dolls and care about them so they learn that discriminatory behaviour causes unhappiness.

Take Natalie as an example:

This is Natalie. She is 4 years old. Like many of you she loves riding her bike, and looking at books. She is a very happy girl. She lives in a caravan.

Have you had a holiday in a caravan or trailer? Do you know anyone who has? I wonder what we know about people who live in a caravan?

Natalie has many similarities to you – can you think what they are? Natalie has some differences to you – I wonder, what are they?

Natalie is called a Traveller. Sometimes she is called a Gypsy. She might come to our school and she might not. If she did, how would we welcome her?

Using persona dolls can help pupils begin to empathise as they put themselves in another person's shoes. If they see the injustice of the situations in the persona doll stories they may think of solutions. Helping to solve the doll's problem can boost children's self-confidence so they are more likely to show respect and sensitivity. After hearing stories in which a doll is unfairly treated, pupils are more likely to have the moral courage to stand up for someone who is excluded, teased or put down.

Persona dolls are being used increasingly in Cumbrian schools to tackle issues of racism and stereotypes. In schools with no ethnic minority pupils they provide a focus for learning to understand and respect children from another culture. In RE lessons they are used as part of an ethnographic approach so pupils can learn about a faith through the experiences recounted by, for instance, a doll with a Muslim or Jewish persona. In schools where negative attitudes towards Travellers have been identified, persona dolls have been particularly useful.

Circles and Cycles for Milo

A Persona doll was used in a rural village school with 60 pupils on role. While Year 6 children were on a residential visit in London, the rest of the pupils were organised into groups of 'families' of mixed age across Reception to Year 5. Teachers planned three theme days during which all cross-curricular work tied into the theme of *Circles and Cycles*. A persona doll was used as the person for whom the work was being done.

Before the theme days the two teachers running the programme devised and memorised the doll's persona. He was to be:

- Yin Meilo (Chinese people usually place their family name first, so we called him Meilo)
- aged 5 (his being young meant if pupils asked him hard questions he could always say he was too young to know the answer)
- born in Beijing, China.
- Meilo speaks Cantonese and knows many words in English. His Dad speaks very good English and his Mum speaks it quite well, though she would like to go to classes to improve.
- He lives here because his Dad has a new job as a scientist at Sellafield, and Meilo and his mum have joined him here. Mum intends to get a job once the family is settled, as she had worked in Beijing.

- In Beijing, Meilo went to school and was taught English. All the children wore a red neckerchief but he doesn't know why.
- His favourite food is noodles and pork.
- He is an only child, as is common in China.
- Meilo is shy and will only talk to the adult holding him.
- While he was with us it became clear that he was uncomfortable with people invading his personal space and touching him without checking if he liked it. (Some pupils were handling him and we used this as an opportunity to discuss this sensitive issue.)

The range of activities around the theme *Circles and Cycles* were all linked to Meilo in some way. The children made furniture just the right size for Meilo from off-cuts of wood and designed wallpaper for Meilo's bedroom in his new house. They made pizza because he hadn't tasted it before (and it is round). They wrote circular stories for Meilo, and made observational drawings of bicycles for Meilo to admire. They had to find out as much as they could about China to tell Meilo (because he was so young he didn't know very much about his home country).

Persona for Mary-Kate – a Gypsy/Traveller doll. This persona was developed specifically for use in an infant school in a town through which many Gypsies and Travellers pass enroute to Appleby Fair

Choice of names: Mary-Kate or Dallas-Kadine, Chanella or Natalia

She has turned 5. She has long dark brown (or black) hair in plaits and green (or brown) eyes.

She is a Romany/English Gypsy and she lives in a trailer (or caravan) with her Mum Melissa, Dad Nathan and baby brother William-Henry (or James-Elisha, or Nicholas). She has two older sisters: Shirelle and Tammy (or Martina, Annie-Martell or Whitney). They sleep in a small trailer beside hers because there wouldn't be room for them all in one trailer.

Her favourite food is her Mum's homemade beef stew but she likes anything her Mum cooks. Sometimes the family have a Chinese take-away for a treat.

Mary-Kate's Dad and her Uncle Joe have a carpet shop but they also travel around the country selling their carpets at fairs and markets. So they aren't always settled in one place, though during the winter they tend to stay in one place.

Her Grandmother makes beautiful silk cushions, pillows and quilts like the ones in Mary-Kate's trailer and she sells them at the fairs. Mum makes beautiful lace-trimmed dresses for little girls and she shares a stall with Gran at the Traveller fairs.

Mary-Kate loves travelling around and stopping at different places. They sometimes stay at Granny and Grandad's Traveller site, especially at Christmas when relatives visit. Granny and Grandad don't travel around much now so they live in a chalet on the site. It was put together in a factory in two pieces and had to be taken to the site on the back of a huge lorry. It looks like a bungalow.

The best days of Mary-Kate's year are: Christmas at Granny and Grandad's; going to Appleby Horse Fair in June to see all the ponies and meet up with lots of family and friends; travelling abroad in the summer when Dad goes to buy the carpets and rugs to sell in his shop.

Mary-Kate likes making new friends when she travels around. She has already been to lots of different schools. The things she liked best at nursery school were painting pictures, playing with the sand and baking biscuits. At her last school she learned how to write her name and soon she hopes to learn how to read. Mary-Kate tries hard not to forget what she learns at school. The teachers often give her some homework to do with Mum while she is travelling.

Some things you will find in Mary-Kate's home are her Mum and Dad's collection of china plates with pictures of horses on them or pictures of fruit, and the glass bowls and vases which have to be wrapped in towels when they move so they don't get broken, and some pretty silk cushions that Granny made and a beautiful Indian rug like the ones her Dad sells.

Outcomes

Using Meilo gave a focus for this project. It drew lots of questions and the children really wanted to find out the answers. They so enjoyed having him visit the school that they were bursting to tell Year 6 all about him when they came back. The pupils' interest in China was significantly boosted.

■ 4.9 Working with a class mascot to support multicultural education

A class mascot, that's a good idea, let's introduce one this coming year.
They can take him home, have lots of fun, and tell us all what they have done.
Speaking and listening will be a breeze, we'll meet our learning goals with ease.
They can bring a picture or photo they took, collect the adventures and make a book.

Armed with the pictures I had the power to make a big book for Literacy Hour!
The book was a hit, the work above par, because in this lesson their bear was the star.
Inspired by this fact Harry did start, in lessons to take an increasing part.
Results were really so much better when Harry taught them to write a letter.

Harry is out in the garden one day, and meets a caterpillar while at play.
He watches as it grows and grows, and waves as off to sleep it goes.
I'll not be a bear, Harry dreamt in bed, I'll be a butterfly instead.
A mat was made and the props were packed into a shiny storysack.
The story was read, the children entranced, learning on this topic really enhanced.

He went on a jet and a rickshaw and liner when he went to visit China.
When he came back, we made a display of things he'd collected along the way,
We counted, made dragons, copied Chinese art, and through it all Harry took part.
We wrote in Chinese, looked at local carving, and the smell of
food made us all starving.

The local paper published a picture, then radio Cumbria arranged a fixture.
Harry told listeners about his role, with the help of two children from our school.

Refreshed and ready to start anew, he was introduced to class number two,
Through a story with a happy end, as Harry was there to be their friend.
He was made in a factory far away, but there he was not long to stay.
Packed in a box and sent by sea, to a shop where Harry thought: 'This isn't for me!'

He jumped off the shelf and on to the floor, took his chance and sped out of the door.
He found a small boat and made a huge leap. Under its canopy he went to sleep.
When he awoke he crept silently out, stood on the grass and looked about.
He made for some buildings up the street, and soon his ears were in for a treat.

Through a window he heard children singing, he felt a glimmer of hope beginning,
As he read a notice on the wall, 'wanted – a class mascot' was the call.
He crept inside by the feet of a Mummy, ignoring the butterflies in his tummy.
Next day their votes the children cast, and Harry had a job at last!

After a trip to Mexico, he rushed back to school raring to go.
He was back in class just after landing to help our knowledge and understanding.
He has jumpers and jackets, slippers and shoes, hats of varying shapes and hues.
A golden crown he was soon to acquire, as to be King Henry he did aspire.

He works very hard for a little bear, helping in class ...or meeting the mayor.
Whether it's English, maths, ICT or PE, it really is very clear to me:
Since Harry to our school came, enrichment has been the name of the game.

Harry has become an integral part of the reception class at an infant school with nearly 100 pupils on role. At the beginning of each year the reception pupils learn about Harry's history and the journey that brought him to their school. The class teacher has photos to show how he came on a boat and walked up to school from the marina. One year the class had a trip to the marina and took clay impressions of the things they – and hence Harry – passed on the way. These were made into plaster casts and displayed in the hall. This special display gives Harry his history.

Harry goes home with one of the pupils each weekend and has a wardrobe of clothes he's gathered over the years. The pupils love taking him home, and when they return him to school they excitedly tell the others about what they did, often bringing photos or drawing a picture. They take *Harry's Book of Adventures* home with them, so the parents can see what it is all about.

Although Harry lives in the reception class, the teacher occasionally does an assembly about his adventures, and if a pupil from another class is going somewhere particularly interesting, he might go with them.

The school was involved in a community arts project with other local schools. All the participants produced art works that were displayed at a special event in the community and the school made banners that feature pictures of Harry.

Harry has been the focus for a number of topic books produced by the class teacher, to add a new dimension to the pupils' learning. These have included a book on caterpillars, earth and space and the seaside, and a rhyming story for English is planned.

With pupils and teachers, Harry has visited other parts of the UK and several countries. The class looks on a map to see where Harry has been, and sometimes a topic about a country is developed after his visit. For example, the pupils had a week of activities on Chinese New Year after Harry visited China. And the parents of the one Chinese boy in the class were able to help with the details. The children looked at pictures and talked about markets, homes, cities and countryside. They did artwork and studied the story of the Willow Pattern. They listened to *The Very Hungry Caterpillar* in Cantonese, finding a few words that sound similar to the English, such as 'pop'. Some phrases are repeated, so the children soon recognised and repeated them. They made Chinese food for a party at the end of the topic.

Harry helping with the China topic display.

The class exchanged emails with children in a school in Hong Kong when a teacher's daughter went to teach there. As a result, the pupils learned about classroom life in Hong Kong and had pictures to look at, some of them featuring Harry. After Harry visited Finland, the class studied reindeers because it was nearly Christmas; after he visited Mexico the class looked at the photos he brought back and played some Mexican instruments; after he visited Ireland they studied Irish coins; and after he visited Scotland they wove tartan patterns, learned Scottish songs and listened to Scottish stories.

The class teacher has ingenious ways for Harry to engage the pupils' interest. For example, when Harry was given a blue and white hat for Christmas it seemed a good idea for him to go to an Everton football match. But the only person going to an Everton match wouldn't take

Harry with part of the mural about how he came to the school.

him. The pupils talked about how disappointed Harry was, and wondered what they could do. They decided to look at the Everton website, found the name of the Chairman and composed an email in literacy hour. The class teacher duly received a phone call from Everton Football Club to say that not only was Harry Bear invited to go to a match but that he could take one of the pupils with him, and go on the pitch and meet the players!

When the class teacher saw an advert for tickets to a Royal Garden Party, the class wrote to Buckingham Palace to say that Harry should be offered a ticket, because he is an ambassador for the school and has travelled all over the world just like the Queen, and would be able to swap tales with her. This got them two tickets to the Royal Garden Party, and they agreed to send a Year 2 pupil, as they thought an older pupil would get more out of it.

Most days Harry sits on the radiator in the classroom. His name is on the register and the children answer for him. As soon as Harry goes home with a pupil for the first weekend of the school year, and reports back afterwards, everyone in the class gets interested. The class learns about the *Harry comes to School* story sometime in the first few weeks of term. He is involved in everyday class activities such as counting songs, and comes to the hall to do PE in his shorts. If a child is upset, the teacher may suggest that Harry sits next to them or reads them a story.

Future plans

This infant school has now merged with two other schools so Harry has retired and a new bear has joined the reception class to start his adventures at the new school. This bear has been photographed helping with building works at the new school site so his own history is being formed. Harry will be used as a mentor for the new bear during a handover period, and he may be kept in retirement in the new school, as a friend for the pupils who remember working with him in their reception year.

Tips for introducing a class mascot

■ Choose your teddy and buy at least three identical spares, so he can be photographed in more than one place at once

■ Customise him to your setting, for example make a jumper out of a school sweatshirt, and provide a nightshirt and nightcap, a toothbrush, and a little teddy

■ Put the teddy and his belongings in a bag with a label and instructions for how he should be looked after when he is taken home or on a trip

■ Construct the teddy's story and family history and prepare a photograph album that reflects it

■ Talk about the teddy at parents' meetings before school starts, using a presentation of pictures from his previous experiences or his life story

■ Take the teddy to meet all the children and parents on the home visits before they join Reception class

■ Talk with the class about things they need and things that make them feel safe if they sleep away from home or go somewhere new

■ Bring the teddy to join in with activities that are daunting for pupils because it makes the pupils feel safer about taking part

■ Take it slowly and let things develop according to the children's reactions. There are many personal and social development issues that come from using a class mascot, and this level of engagement is ideal for developing the mascot's involvement in curriculum topics

I am enthusiastic about this method because I love bears. If you are enthusiastic about what you are doing you will do it better – take it as far as you can, according to how you and the children feel.
Class teacher

■ 4.10: Using a resources box for multicultural education

This project took place in a nursery and infant school with over 300 pupils on role. The school is situated in a town where many of the local people rarely meet people from other countries, so it's not easy to obtain artefacts from other cultures. The class teacher had been a student in Manchester and she started this project by returning to Manchester to buy everyday objects from some of the Chinese and Indian shops she knew there. The shop owners helped gather items that would interest children, especially items not produced for the tourist trade but which ordinary people might buy for regular use.

At this age [reception] any racist attitudes come from parents. They haven't formed them for themselves. We also have some conflict between well-to-do parents and those on the council estates, so we hear children say: 'I'm not playing with him, he's from the council estate'. Or a parent might say that they don't want their child to play with another individual, yet we see that they are good friends at school. This is largely a problem created by the parents.

There's also homophobia in this area, and the typical expectation of men is that they should be butch. If a man stayed at home to look after the

children that would be seen as a negative thing in this area. It is all because of a lack of awareness and education.

So we always write to parents when we're doing a curriculum topic and tell them what the purpose is.
Reception teacher

The reception teacher has found that when young children are introduced to other countries many of them are more interested in the animals than the people. She says:

It is our job to introduce the people who live in other countries and this is why I've gathered up resource boxes of everyday things to show them. Reception children are very open and it is easy to underestimate their ability to understand. Around the age of five or six a child is forming 50% of their knowledge and children of this age are surprising in what they remember. Generally they have not yet developed stereotypes about other countries, unless they come from home backgrounds where these are picked up. Sometimes a child will use racist language. They are just getting to the age where their ideas are being affected by outside influences.

The reception class did a Big Wide World topic based around a central focus of a wall display. They played with plastic snakes in the sand tray and crocodiles in the water tray. The plastic creatures interested the active boys, unlike other classroom activities such as dressing up and painting. The teacher explained the names of some countries the animals came from and brought a wider dimension to the topic by using her resource boxes.

In the India Box there were

- girls' bangles
- book of postcards
- story book in Hindi
- colourful papier-mâché box
- packet of incense
- stories by Indian authors
- colourful wedding garlands
- bottle of henna
- bottle of men's hair oil
- leaflet explaining how to wear a sari
- parchment paper printed with a calendar
- information about a school's environmental activities (produced for sale by an Indian school)
- samples of materials
- poster about Divali

A few reception pupils at a time were introduced to the resource box. Each pupil was asked to choose an item they liked and describe it. The group discussed what each chosen item might be used for and what it was made from. Some pupils chose to draw a picture of their item, producing some accurately observed representational drawings. Some were motivated to bring their own bracelets and necklaces into school.

There were further opportunities to work with the patterns found on the cloth and craft items, and for pupils to make their own patterns in a similar style. Pupils learned that people in different countries often have similar things, even though their cultures are different.

Toys

When the staff from this school and their friends go abroad they are asked to bring back toys. These form a collection which supports the Toys topic in Reception. The collection includes South American and Caribbean dolls, and these invite comparison of materials because they are made of wood and cloth, not plastic. The collection also includes photographs of children in a range of countries playing with similar toys while wearing clothes similar to those of children in the UK. So the pupils see that not everything in other countries differs. There is a photograph of children in Peru with their family's llamas, and this is used with a toy llama made of wool for the pupils to hold and talk about. The pupils visited a local animal park and the llama farm, to see these animals in a real context.

The class starts the topic on Toys by sharing a story about another country, and this leads into whole class discussion. There is a choice of activities throughout the day, allowing small groups to look at the toy collection. The pupils are taught to handle the items

delicately. Some groups spend up to half an hour examining the toys in detail because they are so engaged. Children build homes for the toys and animals from sand or stones, or look at books with pictures of people in other countries and then draw some of them.

In this reception class topics are cross-curricular, so the study of another country involves counting rhymes for numeracy, stories from the country for literacy, art, craft and music activities, and some geography. The teacher tries to introduce different cultures in a range of topics. When the pupils were drawing faces on their cress yoghurt pots, the teacher noticed that they were all colouring pink faces. She showed the class pictures of people from various ethnic groups and said, 'Now decide what colour skin to draw'.

Outcomes

When asked to share their news, one child said: '*I went to London*' and then remarked: '*I saw lots of people with brown faces*'. The class discussed the fact that there are people of many cultures and with various skin colours in the UK and that it is okay to talk about skin colour if it's done respectfully. Another pupil contributed to the discussion: '*There were two Chinese children on the roller-coaster at Blackpool, they were talking just the same as us!*' These moments are important. When children's interest is sparked, and reflected in a statement or question, they are ready to pursue it, consider it, make mental links and move their understanding on.

This age group don't conceive of other places in an adult way, but the teacher can offer a context and memories they can connect as they begin to understand more.

Future plans

The school has started a link with a rural school in the western Lake District. They visited each other so the pupils experienced the similarities and differences between a large urban school and a small rural one. The reception teacher is keen to tackle some of the stereotypes held about Cumbria, as well as about other countries. This school is in a socially deprived urban area and some pupils never visit the Lake District National Park, yet many people assume that everyone in Cumbria lives in an idyllic rural situation surrounded by sheep and lakes. Linking with another school helps pupils understand what other places are like, even places nearby, so they learn that not everywhere is the same as where they live.

Section 5
How do we evaluate and reflect?
How do we move on from just celebrating cultures?

Teachers need to use proactive teaching and learning strategies to challenge pupils' attitudes. It is not enough to sample other cultures. We need to make sure we haven't just moved from doing saris, samosas and steel bands to drums, printing and maize dolls. This section gives teachers tools for reflecting on the work in their school and tackling the difficult issues. It focuses on projects which challenge prejudice and tackle racism as well as celebrating multiculturalism.

Multicultural education has been criticised for 'celebrating diversity and difference whilst leaving the structures of racism intact. (David Gillborn)

Much has been written on the main differences between multicultural and antiracist education approaches. Stella Dadzie in *Tools for Tackling Racism in Schools* (Trentham, 1999) summarises the drawbacks of multicultural education:

■ *It may imply that cultural differences, rather than racism, are 'the problem'*

■ *It may assume that the dominant culture is the norm to which others should conform or be compared*

■ *It can encourage a 'zoo mentality' by emphasising the exotic or curious*

■ *It may reinforce existing prejudices based on stereotypical representations of other cultures, religions and lifestyles*

■ *It may overlook questions of economic or ideological power and social hierarchy which are central to understanding racism*

■ *It can make the majority group feel they have no culture – that only ethnic minority groups have culture.*

Activities taking place in two schools illustrate some of the differences between an antiracist and a multicultural approach (see page 44/85).

This school delivers multicultural education

■ It includes cooking, music, dances and traditional 'costumes' (not clothes) from around the world.

■ It holds Africa and Asia weeks with African and Asian artists.

■ It displays images of a multicultural world around the school.
■ Other localities are studied without existing assumptions being challenged.

■ It teaches about the major world religions through celebrating Eid and Divali alongside Christian festivals.
■ It takes pupils on a visit to a Hindu temple.

This school delivers antiracist education

■ It embeds antiracist education throughout the whole curriculum, not only in citizenship, PSHE, RE or English.

■ All teachers, support staff and pupils use the words 'some'; 'many' 'or most' before naming a cultural or religious group e.g. 'some Germans' or 'many Hindus'.

■ It holds a Ghana culture week as the focus for work throughout the curriculum for one term and as a stimulus for antiracist work.

■ Staff use resources in the curriculum, such as the *Throwing Stones* video pack from Leicestershire Constabulary; *Moral Courage* from the Anne Frank Trust or *Coming Unstuck* from Hampshire LEA.

■ Staff and pupils check all displays, jigsaws, and books for non-stereotypical images of contemporary multicultural Britain, and one criterion for purchasing is whether new resources reflect diversity.

■ Teachers introduce the study of another locality with honest discussions about assumptions and expectations, so as to acknowledge prejudice and challenge stereotypes.

■ Specific religions are taught in such a way that pupils learn 'What it might be like to be ...Jewish, Muslim, Buddhist' etc and the day-to-day life of faith groups, not just the festivals.

■ Teachers distinguish clearly between cultural lifestyle and religious observance.

■ Diversity within Christianity is used as a basis for exploring diversity within other religions.

■ The experience of what it might be like to be a persecuted member of a faith or culture is explored.

■ Pupils have email links with pupils at a school near a Hindu temple so they visit it together and have ongoing email communication.

This school delivers multicultural education

■ It has a school link with Africa to sponsor children to go to school, and holds regular fundraising activities as well as penfriending.

■ Race equality is included as part of the school anti-bullying policy.
■ One or two teachers have been on multicultural courses but most staff have not received race equality training.

■ Little provision is made for ethnic minority pupils and no provision for Traveller pupils.
■ Teachers with ethnic minority and Traveller pupils in their class often resent the extra work and have no time to access appropriate training.

This school delivers antiracist education

■ It has a partnership link with a school in Ghana.
■ In addition to penfriend letters, classes exchange project work on rivers and locality for geography; the experience of colonisation and colonialism for history; and activities on children's rights for PSHE and citizenship.

■ Twice a month the linked schools share the results of their Philosophy for Children enquiries, after using similar starting points.

■ Any money raised is for teacher exchanges to take place.

■ After receiving whole school race equality training the school developed a Race Equality Policy and Action Plan, in consultation with mid-day supervisors, site supervisor, secretary, teachers, teaching assistants, governors, parents and pupils.

■ The policy includes procedures for dealing with and monitoring racist incidents; for recruitment; and for monitoring ethnic minority pupils' achievement.

■ Race equality training is an essential condition of service for all staff.

■ A proactive school council has taken the lead in the development of a pupil version of the Race Equality Policy

■ Teachers access appropriate materials and training and they analyse achievement data of ethnic minority pupils to make sure they are achieving their full potential.
■ Methodologies used throughout the curriculum encourage children to think deeply and skilfully so they can give meaningful reasons for their opinions and work collaboratively.

■ The school ethos effectively develops personal self-esteem and self-respect as well as respect for difference.

5.1: Evaluating classroom practice and whole school approaches

Teachers need to reflect on and evaluate the activities, curriculum work and special events taking place in school to get a clear picture of how effectively everyday class teaching is incorporating multicultural and antiracist issues.

Start by choosing any recent activity in your class from any curriculum area, for example the role play area, a literacy lesson or a science topic. Consider what the pupils learned about:

- being a girl or being a boy
- families
- their own culture
- other communities
- disability
- ethnic and cultural groups
- their own community
- similarities and differences

Questions for all staff to examine our existing practices

1. How would you introduce into your school:

   a Gypsy/ Traveller child?
   a Muslim child?
   a refugee child?
   a child using a wheelchair?

2. Which children might be rejected by others in our school?

3. How would you tackle an incident of prejudice? of discrimination? of rejection?

4. To what extent should we foster a sense of local identity?

5. How might you address a child's unconscious arrogance about their identity?

6. In some schools Black and Asian adults have been well received while visiting in a professional or official capacity but abused when walking across the playground or down the street. What would you do about it in our school?

Creating a questioning environment

A Cumbrian teacher describes her approach:

As pupils come into the classroom each morning I make sure that there is some world music playing. They have 'Listening Diaries' in which they write their thoughts and impressions of the music. I write a 'Question for the Day' on the whiteboard for children to reflect on – for instance: 'Should children always listen to adults?'; 'Does everyone have a right to an education?'; 'Should all people be treated equally?' They get engrossed in discussing the question in small groups while I deal with the morning routines – registration etc. We've had some excellent discussions and most pupils now feel it is okay to change their mind about a previously strongly held view.

We regularly use *Newswise* by Roger Sutcliffe of SAPERE as the stimulus for an in depth Philosophy for Children (P4C) enquiry. For instance when I used the autumn 2005 edition on 'National Hero' I really didn't know what to expect from my new class but was delighted by the interest shown. Indeed, three days later, one girl was spotted researching 'Tebbit's Test' on the Internet in her free time! Another girl explained how she had introduced the ideas about a loyalty test for immigrants at home which ended with the whole family discussing the merits of whether such a test would result in knowing who was loyal or not. After the P4C enquiry used the *Newswise* stimulus, I asked the pupils what they thought of it. Comments included: 'Fascinating'; 'I learnt a lot'; 'Amazing to think you could be regarded as British by which team you support'; and 'It's made me think what it means to 'belong'. I was inundated with questions especially as I had lived so long in other countries. They asked me whether I supported their teams when I was there or not and whether I should support them if I lived there and what it meant to live in another country.

Checklist for reflecting on and evaluating antiracist and multicultural activities

Questions to ask yourself	Which activity?	Comments
What worked? How do you know?		
How will you sustain this activity so it isn't tokenistic?		
How did staff attitudes during the activity affect pupils' understanding and experiences?		
When will you be returning to this activity?		
How will you share the learning from this activity with other children in school and with the community?		
How did the activity work with families to raise equality and diversity issues at home as well as in school?		
Did the activity present a balanced view, for example the space programme in India as well as the poverty?		
Did the activity offer opportunities for pupils to detect bias, for example by scrutinising newspaper reports, and to recognise and challenge stereotypes, for example when using photos?		
Did you answer children's questions and concerns and not imply that certain things (e.g. somebody's skin colour) should not be mentioned?		
Did the activity help pupils to enjoy differences rather than fear them, and help them understand that people have more similarities than differences?		
Did you use examples of the contributions made by a range of cultural and ethnic groups e.g. Travellers?		
Did this activity show that people have many things in common but also different heritages, so their ways of looking at the world might differ?		
Did you use resources and books which show people from a range of societies and backgrounds and give positive models of a range of ethnic groups?		
What methods did you use to help children learn the skill of politely challenging opinions and sensitively confronting negative attitudes?		
How did the activity explore global issues and interdependence, such as where things come from and about the people who make them?		
How did the activity inspire pupils with the idea that they can make a difference and that institutions can be used to make change happen?		

■ 5.2: We're doing a week about... guidelines on culture weeks

Holding an intensive week of activities that focus on a specific country has proved an exciting way to promote awareness and understanding of cultural diversity and a basis for exploring prejudice and stereotypes. A whole school approach offering a range of curriculum activities allows pupils to extend their knowledge of other people's lifestyles and develop new skills. Pupils experience the music, art, literature, stories or dance of a country at first hand and meet people from different cultural backgrounds. Many agencies, artists, dancers, musicians, poets and writers provide resources and performances to enhance the curriculum in this way.

However, great care is needed to ensure that the good intentions are realised, racial stereotypes are not confirmed and perceptions of other countries aren't narrow or superficial.

Country versus continent

Don't confuse a country with a continent containing many countries, climates, economic systems and ethnic groups. The continent of Africa, with its 53 countries, is so big it could contain the whole of Europe, North America and China. Activities need to raise awareness of a particular country, culture, festival or event, rather than a generality.

Stereotypical images versus balanced view

Many of the resources available to schools from charities may show images of deprivation, poverty, lack of modern technology and people who need help. Compounded by media images, they can leave pupils believing that everyone in Africa is poor, covered in flies, unsmiling and carrying things on their heads. Even when pupils know the word 'stereotype' they often still make generalisations like 'people in Africa are poor'. Creating a balanced view might mean having discussions about Nigerians who own jumbo jets, or showing pictures of rich people in Ghana outside their houses or high-rise flats.

A Cumbrian teacher who uses P4C regularly with her class, described the effect a Primary Enterprise Project workshop had on her Year 6 class topic of 'Our World', where pupils were introduced to trade between countries.

> It has been a real eye-opener for them. Some are making connections between the war in Iraq and the presence of oil in Iraq! They want to know why US intervention doesn't also happen in Cambodia or North Korea or Ethiopia. Some are seeing there are no material gains for rich countries in these war-torn or controlled places. It is really good seeing them think for themselves.

Culture versus religion

Religious observance is a reflection of faith. Not everyone living in a society that has a dominant religion practises it, although aspects of their lives may be influenced by that religion. So pupils need help understanding that just as not everyone in England is a practicing Christian, not everyone in India is a practicing Hindu or Muslim. Up-to-date materials and information are essential, and magazines and newspapers can help give a flavour of everyday life in a country.

Chinese New Year display.

'Many', 'some' and 'few' versus 'everybody'

Pupils need to learn not to assume that all people do what they see a few doing or to generalise that everyone from a country or faith believes or does the same things. For example, not all people in England eat fish and chips, many like drinking tea, some take pride in their gardens and a few enjoy train spotting. Not all people in Africa play the drums and dance. 'Many', some' or 'a few' should always precede any mention of a national or faith groups, for example many Pakistanis; some Americans; a few Muslims.

Whatever the age group, activities during a culture week should begin with the pupils reflecting on their existing views of the culture before they start to learn more about it. Stereotypes need to be voiced so misinformation isn't perpetuated. Do the English all eat sausage and mash, wear ties to work, and read Beatrix Potter? Elements of white English culture should be included in culture weeks, as knowledge and understanding of their own culture and community helps children to develop a sense of belonging and a strong self image.

Culture weeks can be more than just fun and celebration. Some schools settle for colourful art work, dancing and singing but avoid issues of prejudice and discrimination. In other schools teachers generate reflection and discussion with such questions as: '*If someone from this culture walked through our village or moved in next door to you, what would be the reaction?*'

A culture week can be a way into antiracist education if it is used to move on to deeper issues. However some teachers with responsibility for equality become frustrated by the superficial practice of colleagues. As one said:

> *I couldn't believe it. All they wanted to do was get children to make 'African' masks. When I asked them 'Which country in Africa are we going to focus on?' they didn't want to engage. They said: 'There isn't time to research it to that depth, let's just do this lovely activity'. Yet when a Reception child burst into tears at her first sight of the 'African drummer' (from Sierra Leone) staff found it hard to deal with the issues raised.*

Experiences in Cumbrian schools suggest five important principles for culture weeks

■ The whole staff team need to plan together so progression is clear

■ Someone from the culture needs to inspire and lead planning and launch the week

■ Plenty of artefacts must be available so all the senses are engaged and experiences are hands on, especially for younger children

■ Resources need to be pooled in a box in the staff room so staff can dip into them during the week

■ During the subsequent week an exhibition should display the full range of what the children have done and parents and grandparents invited to share the excitement of the work. Culturally appropriate snacks and drinks can be served and a DVD shown of the activities during the week.

Common mistakes to avoid

Africa is not a country and doesn't have one culture.

Animal masks are not necessarily appropriate. They may be sold to tourists, but not worn by ordinary people. It depends on which part of which country.

People in African countries wear a huge diversity of clothes.

Effective multicultural and anti-racist education doesn't just focus on differences.

Pupils have been making a noise about Africa after spending the week learning about the country and its culture.

Pupils took part in a series of activities, from music to mask-making to cooking and dancing, as part of a multicultural curriculum exercise.

The Year 5 teacher said they had to look at a third world country and they chose to study black Africa. Youngsters made musical instruments, listened to traditional African music and played their own, made brightly coloured animal and tribal masks and costumes and even sampled African dishes including a chicken stew-type dish with couscous.

"They thoroughly enjoyed it. It was something they didn't know about before and they didn't appreciate how different things are over there" said the class teacher.

Report from a Cumbrian school's culture week which appeared in a local newspaper.

Just learning about music and food is shallow and stereotypical, it is not 'learning about the country'.

Each country in Africa has its own traditions and cultures. Making costumes and masks is not an appropriate way to learn about other cultures.

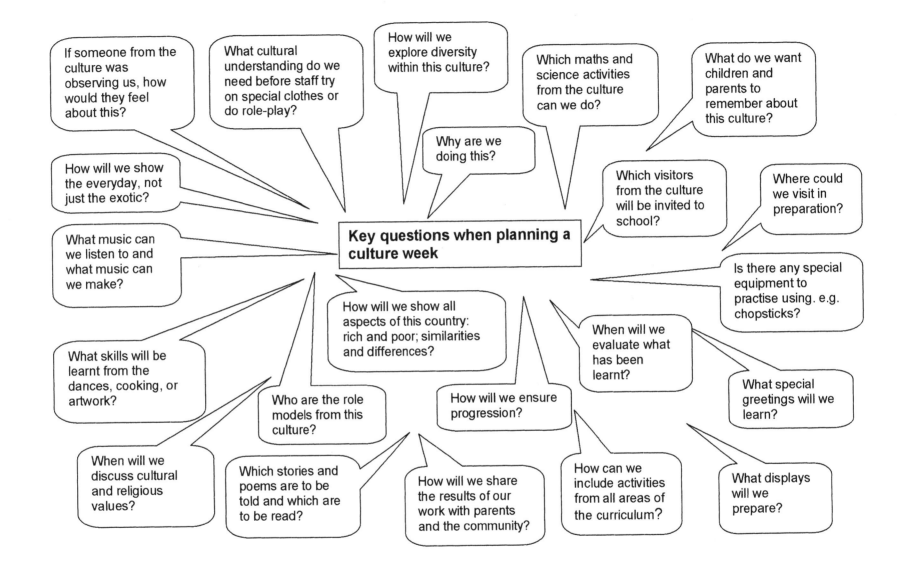

Key questions when planning a culture week

If someone from the culture was observing us, how would they feel about this?

What cultural understanding do we need before staff try on special clothes or do role-play?

How will we explore diversity within this culture?

Which maths and science activities from the culture can we do?

What do we want children and parents to remember about this culture?

Why are we doing this?

How will we show the everyday, not just the exotic?

What music can we listen to and what music can we make?

Which visitors from the culture will be invited to school?

Where could we visit in preparation?

Is there any special equipment to practise using. e.g. chopsticks?

What skills will be learnt from the dances, cooking, or artwork?

How will we show all aspects of this country: rich and poor; similarities and differences?

When will we evaluate what has been learnt?

What special greetings will we learn?

Who are the role models from this culture?

How will we ensure progression?

When will we discuss cultural and religious values?

Which stories and poems are to be told and which are to be read?

How will we share the results of our work with parents and the community?

How can we include activities from all areas of the curriculum?

What displays will we prepare?

■ 5.3: Using books in antiracist and multicultural education

Texts which match the requirements of the Primary National Strategy and value cultural diversity can be starting points for exploring prejudice. Books can be used to raise issues for discussion in positive ways to broaden pupils' experiences of cultural diversity and to challenge racism. Such material needs to be introduced to very young children and built on each year so issues of progression are addressed.

But it is not just a matter of having the books on the shelves. There is a danger that some approaches to multiculturalism in the Primary National Strategy may lead to tokenism. If a text is used in literacy without being followed up with constructive dialogue and questioning, it can confirm stereotypes. The challenge is to use a text as a springboard for antiracist work in a range of curriculum areas such as PSHE, citizenship, geography, RE and IT. Race equality needs to be integrated into all aspects of school life – no area of the curriculum is neutral.

Ofsted recommends that every classroom should have a range of texts in different scripts so that even young children begin to appreciate that there are many languages. We need to examine books critically and select those which reflect a balanced picture of our multiethnic society and show positive images of people from a range of cultures, in everyday situations and activities. The following questions should be asked about the texts we already have, and whenever new purchases are considered. (See Section 4.3 and 4.4 for ideas on using story books as a stimulus for philosophical enquiry.)

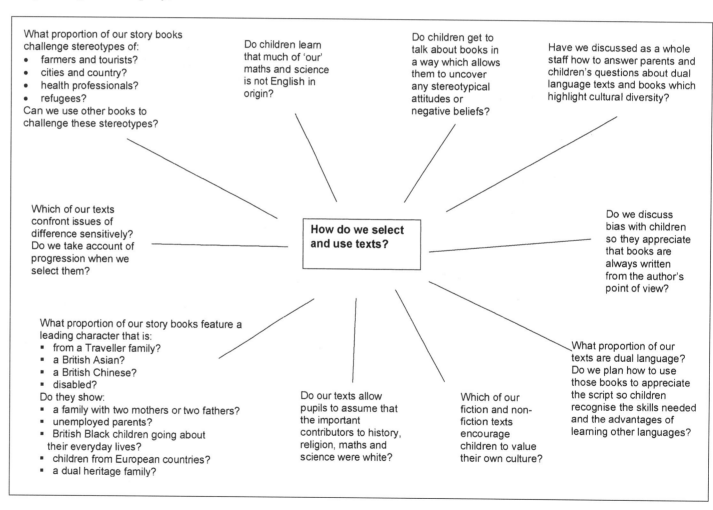

What proportion of our story books challenge stereotypes of:
- farmers and tourists?
- cities and country?
- health professionals?
- refugees?

Can we use other books to challenge these stereotypes?

Do children learn that much of 'our' maths and science is not English in origin?

Do children get to talk about books in a way which allows them to uncover any stereotypical attitudes or negative beliefs?

Have we discussed as a whole staff how to answer parents and children's questions about dual language texts and books which highlight cultural diversity?

Which of our texts confront issues of difference sensitively? Do we take account of progression when we select them?

How do we select and use texts?

Do we discuss bias with children so they appreciate that books are always written from the author's point of view?

What proportion of our story books feature a leading character that is:
- from a Traveller family?
- a British Asian?
- a British Chinese?
- disabled?

Do they show:
- a family with two mothers or two fathers?
- unemployed parents?
- British Black children going about their everyday lives?
- children from European countries?
- a dual heritage family?

Do our texts allow pupils to assume that the important contributors to history, religion, maths and science were white?

Which of our fiction and non-fiction texts encourage children to value their own culture?

What proportion of our texts are dual language? Do we plan how to use those books to appreciate the script so children recognise the skills needed and the advantages of learning other languages?

■ 5.4: Using artefacts from other cultures and places

When teachers use artefacts to engage pupils in a process of discovery about another culture, it is important to not fix attention only on the outward object. Artefacts must not be merely shown, described and drawn. As objects they are dumb; as artefacts used in context, they speak.

An artefact needs a context: facts, stories, discussion, exploring any symbolism, the craftsmanship, how it is used, and the feelings of those who use it. Teachers should not focus only on the externals of the artefact and its use, but ask questions like:

> *What does this mean to the person who uses it or to the person who made it?*
>
> *How might it affect their life?*
>
> *What beliefs or concepts does this artefact point to?*
>
> *How does this relate to me?*

How do we use artefacts to develop respect?

Pupils may need practice in talking about things in a positive way and asking questions such as 'How is it used?' and 'What does it mean?' A sense of respect must be built, so that pupils treat artefacts with care. These objects matter to somebody, whether or not they have monetary value. Teachers could introduce a preliminary exercise so pupils practise carefully handling objects, gently passing round an egg, or a tambourine without making a sound, or mime picking up a wounded bird.

Start by developing pupils' understanding of special objects. Show pupils something that has great value to you because of its symbolic, not monetary, value and explain why. This might be a photo, a pressed flower, an entrance ticket. Discuss other things that are precious that may have no monetary value, such as a shell or an old teddy bear.

Have a circle time round of 'If my home was on fire, all the people and animals were safe and I could rescue one thing, it would be...', or 'I would hate to lose my...', or 'I would be angry if somebody spoilt my....'. Show a picture of refugees and ask 'If you had to leave home quickly and couldn't carry much, what one thing would you want to take to remind you of home.'

Ask pupils:

> Do you have a special object?
>
> What object is most special to your family?
>
> Where do you keep it?
>
> When do you use it?
>
> What makes it special? Would you lend it, to whom and why?

Invite pupils to bring their special object to school if possible, to make a display of special things. Discuss how we should treat other people's special objects. Pupils could write a poem on 'The object I love above all others...' or 'Don't ever throw out my...'. Or they could contribute to a collage of drawings of 'Things we have loved'.

Ask pupils if they know any objects used by the people whose culture you are learning about. Where do they keep them? When do they use them? What makes them special?

Teachers need to prepare carefully so they use the correct terminology and can anticipate pupils' questions. They need to treat each artefact with respect and introduce objects with care to prevent ridicule or instant negative judgements. To encourage empathy the artefact should be used in the same way as those to whom culturally it belongs. Ask pupils to reflect on the feelings of those who use it and on whether there is anything in their own life that is like it.

Show an artefact as a lesson starter, to raise interest; encourage questions and extend thinking. Don't give a talk on the culture first – let the artefact be the enticer. Or to spark imagination, use in a feely-bag or mystery bag:

What is in the feely bag?

1. Just by feeling carefully and without looking into the bag try to answer these questions:

- What does the object feel like?
- What do you think the object is?
- What use might it have?
- From what do you think it is made?
- What would you like to know about it?

2. Now take the object out of the bag and see if you can answer these questions:

- How might the object be used?   Who might use it?
- When might it be used?   Why might it be used?
- What other questions would you like answering?

Encourage pupils to question and problem solve by giving an artefact to each group and asking them to:

Look closely at your artefact:

- Describe it. What do you think it is? Who do you think might use it?
- How might it be used? When might it be used? Where might it be used?
- Why might it be important to the person using it? What culture might it come from?
- How many different questions can you ask about your artefact? Write them down.
- Pass your questions and artefact to another group, who will try to find the answers.

Each group can report back to explain what they found out about the artefact – what it is, how it is used, and the importance it has to those who use it.

Show pupils two examples of the same artefact and ask them to list the similarities and differences. What are the essential elements?

To help pupils remember correct terminology for artefacts from a culture play Kim's Game. Group several artefacts on a tray, cover with a cloth, remove one and ask pupils to name the missing object.

Pupils could make a replica artefact in order to begin to appreciate its importance to a particular community.

The learning process of using an artefact from another culture should be in five stages:

- Introduce the artefact gradually
- Children describe what they see, perhaps using comparisons
- Children ask questions about it
- Children find the answers to their questions from a range of sources
- Children reflect on any significance in their own lives

The learning outcomes of using an artefact from another culture should be that pupils understand:

- what it is
- how it is used
- what value and importance it has for those who use it

Without this understanding pupils may dismiss artefacts from other cultures as 'weird' or 'funky'.

Artefacts available for loan from CDEC

■ 5.5 Using images of other cultures and places

The most powerful influences on us as learners are vivid concrete images. A large part of the brain's sensory input comes from visual sources so well-chosen photos and posters can be extremely effective in raising questions and shaping understanding of other cultures and places. There are many Development Education photo-packs, or search on Google Images (www.google.co.uk) to find photos which can be downloaded and used in a range of ways to support well-planned antiracist projects in schools.

Photopacks available on loan from CDEC.

To investigate images what questions should we ask?

1. What can you see here?

2. What is the main focus of this picture?

3. What ideas are expressed in this picture?

4. Does this picture arouse any feelings in you? Has the content anything to do with you?

5. Does this picture raise any questions about life for you?

1. How can we encourage pupils to ask questions about photos?

■ For each group paste a photo onto a large piece of paper and ask pupils to write as many questions and observations as possible around it.

■ Display a selection of photos around the room so that pupils can choose the one they like best, explain why, and write down the questions they would most like to have answered about it.

■ Pupils rank the photos they like best in a diamond shape, starting with the one they like the most, and thinking about their reasons. They write their own caption for the photo they like the most and note down the questions they would most like to have answered about it.

Look closely at your photo:

Describe everything you can see in the photo.

What do you think is going on?

Describe what you think happened ten minutes before the photo was taken and what might happen ten minutes afterwards.

How many different questions can you ask about your photo? Write them down.

Pass your questions to another group and ask them to try to find the answers to your questions while you find the answers to their questions.

Each group reports back to explain what they have found out about the photo.

Describe why you think the photographer took this particular photo.

Draw a comic strip story about the event in your photo.

2. How can we encourage observation of similarities between people from different cultures or religions?

■ In groups, pupils choose their own categories into which to organise a selection of photos, such as all those showing women; groups of people; people outside; the most surprising photos; the photos that give the most information.

■ Give each group three photos: one taken locally, one from another part of Britain and one from overseas. Ask pupils to find common themes between the photos (for example, everyone is smiling, or praying). Allow time to discover unusual categories.

Photo from CDEC collections

3. How can we encourage observation of differences between cultures or religions?

■ In groups, pupils select two photos they think are different and explain to the other groups the ways they differ.

■ Pupils choose pairs of photos which are contrasting, such as many people or few people, city or countryside.

4. How can we help pupils understand that photos are part of a much bigger picture?

■ In pairs children answer the following questions about a photo:

Why do you think the photo was taken?
Who do you think took it?
Who is it appealing to?
What do you think is going on just outside the photo?

■ Give each group a small part of a photocopy of a photo and ask them to draw in the missing parts of the picture. Show them the complete photo, discuss their ideas and that there is more to any picture than we can see.

5. How can we help pupils learn that the way we 'see' photos can be influenced by its caption?

■ In pairs, pupils make up their own captions for a set of photos, before matching captions that the teacher or other pupils have written to the photos.

■ Present the same photos with one positive and one negative caption (for example, 'The classrooms in the mosque are not well equipped', or 'Muslim women have the chance to study'. Discuss which caption is positive and which negative, and how a caption can change the meaning.

■ Give each group one copy of the same photo and write a different brief for each group. The briefs could be:

You are designing a calendar of religions or cultures around the world

You are making a poster to raise money to help these people

You are designing a recipe book of religious or cultural food

You are a journalist researching this religion or culture

You are a journalist covering a story showing how these people are helpful

Photo from CDEC collections.

Each group then writes a positive and a negative caption for the photo according to their brief.

Discuss how the meaning of a photo can change according to its caption, and how negative captions can affect the way we see the people and their culture.

6. How can we encourage pupils to ask 'What is this culture or religion really like?'

■ Place photos which have been pasted onto larger pieces of paper around the room. Give each pupil a sticker on which to write their initials. Ask pupils to put their sticker next to the photo they find the most interesting, for whatever reason. Pupils who picked the same photo should work as a group to discuss why they chose the photo and what they would like to ask about it.

Photo from CDEC collections.

■ In groups, select two photos.

With the first photo: Imagine you are one of the people in the photo. What are you thinking? What are you doing? What do you want? What is your life like? What are you saying? Write down your thoughts.

With the second photo: Think about the photo and what is happening. What is the photo about? What is going on? Where are the people? What is their daily life like? What is happening? What would you like to know about the people and places in the photo? Write your questions around the photo.

7. How can we help develop pupil's awareness of diversity in their own area?

Each group selects a photo of a person they would like to email or phone to find out about the beliefs in the local area. How much might this person already know? How would they know? How would you describe your area if you were trying to encourage them to come and visit you? Would you leave anything out? Discuss how much they think they know about the person in the photo.

8. How do we help pupils realise that we don't always notice the things we see?

■ Select a photo which has a lot going on in it. Send five pupils out of the room. Show the class the photo and ask one pupil (Pupil A) to study it for a minute. Hide the photo and invite one pupil (Pupil B) back into the room. Pupil A should describe the photo as fully as possible. Based on that description, Pupil B describes it to the next pupil to come in, and so on till all five have been given a description of the photo. Compare the description the last pupil receives with the photo itself. How did the image change? Were any assumptions made? Why?

■ Pupils work in pairs. Pupil A looks at a photo for one minute, then places it face down and describes it to pupil B, who draws what is being described. Pupil B does the same with pupil A, using a different photo. What things were described well and why? What was left out and why? This can be adapted so children look at the photo while they describe it.

■ Children sit back-to-back with a partner and one describes a photo from a selection they have been using, while the other tries to guess which photo it is and what is happening.

■ Section 5.6: Contacts and Resources

Contacts

Albie Ollivierre
African-Caribbean dance
Flat 96, Clare House, 10 Hawthorn Ave,
Bow, London E3 5PZ
Tel: 07903 211924 or 07951 091984

Anne Frank Trust
Star House, 104-108 Grafton Road,
London NW5 4BA
Tel: 020 7284 5858
info@annefrank.org.uk

British Council
Comenius Programme
www.britishcouncil.org/socrates.nbm

Commission for Racial Equality
www.cre.gov.uk/publs/catalogue
Free posters available

Cumbria Development Education Centre
(CDEC)
St Martin's College (Kelsick Annexe)
Ambleside, Cumbria LA22 9BB
Tel: 015394 30231
Email: cdec@ucsm.ac.uk

Cumbria Education Service
Kendal Office, Busher Walk,
Kendal, Cumbria, LA9 4RQ
www.cumbria.gov.uk

Durham and Darlington Traveller
Education Service
Broom Cottages Primary & Nursery
School
Ferryhill, Co. Durham DL17 8AN
Tel: 01740 656998 Fax: 01740 657792
email: freda.fielding@durham.gov.uk

Forum Theatre
www.cardboardcitizens.co.uk

Global Link
24a New Street, Lancaster LA1 1EG
Tel: 01524 36201
www.globallink.org.uk

Lancashire Global Education Centre
37 St Peter's Square, Preston PR1 7BX
Tel: 01772 252299
www.lgec.org.uk

Letterbox Library
Celebrating equality and diversity in
children's books
71-73 Allen Road, Stoke Newington,
London N16 8RY
Tel: 0207 503 4801 Fax: 0207 503 4800
Email: info@letterboxlibrary.com
www.letterboxlibrary.com

Lip Lee
Chinese artist
21 Holmside Place, Heaton, Newcastle-
upon-Tyne NE6 5AJ
Tel: 0191 265 8071
lip-lee@tinyworld.co.uk

Oxfam
A range of Global Citizenship and
development education teaching
resources
www.oxfam.org.uk/coolplanet/kidsweb/
index.htm

Persona Dolls
Persona Doll Training
51 Granville Rd, London N12 OJH
personadoll@ukgateway.net
www.persona-doll-training.org

Society for the Advancement of
Philosophical Enquiry and Reflection in
Education (SAPERE)
Westminster Institute of Education,
Oxford Brookes University,
Harcourt Hill Campus, Oxford, OX2 9AT
Tel: 01865 488340
Email: admin@sapere.net
www.sapere.org.uk

Resources mentioned in the text

Africans in Tudor Britain
The Ethnic Minority Achievement
Service, Lancashire County Council

*Alphabet Photo Frieze of Children Around
the World*
NES Arnold, £9.99

Beegu
Alexis Deacon, Red Fox, 2004

Birthday Party
Nelson Thornes 2001, Stepping Stones,
Unit 1 Week 1, Birthday Party, Ourselves

Britain – We all make it Unique
A4 poster produced by the Commission
for Racial Equality, Free.
ISBN 185442 316 9

*Combating Discrimination – Persona
dolls in action*
Babette Brown, Trentham Books, 2001

*Coming Unstuck: Teaching about racism
with 10 to 11-year-olds*
Hampshire LEA, Winchester Local
Education Office

Cumbrian Attitudes 2004
Cumbria County Council and Cumbria
Constabulary, January 2005
www.cumbria.gov.uk

Elmer
David McKee, Red Fox, 1990

*Gypsy and Traveller Picture Library – to
promote race equality An essential pack of
photographs on four themed CDs*
Durham and Darlington Traveller
Education Service

A Horse for Joe
Margaret Hird and Ann Whitwell,
Wiltshire County Council
Available from The Willsden Bookshop
www.willsdenbookshop.co.uk

I Wish I Didn't Have To Sleep
Keith Hamel, Prestel, 1997

Lancashire Cumbria Photopack
Cumbria Development Education Centre
and Global Link

Moral Courage – who's got it? Video
Anne Frank Trust

*My Wonderful Place: the story of a journey
to Appleby Fair*
Sally Barter, London Borough of
Hillingdon Traveller Education Service

Newswise
Classroom resource to develop critical
thinking – 6 issues per year
Available from Roger Sutcliffe, SAPERE
rogersutcliffe@onet.co.uk

Philosophy for Six Year Olds
BBC Transformers video

The Skin I'm In
Pat Thomas, Barron's Educational Series,
2003

Something Else
Kathryn Cave, Puffin, 1995

That's My Mum
Henriette Barkow, Mantra Publishing,
2001

*A Time to Look Back: Appleby Fair over
the last 50 years*
Published by Barrie Law

*A Time to Remember: A Collection of
photographs of the travelling people and
their way of life*
published by Barrie Law

*Throwing Stones: An anti-racist teaching
guide and video for Key Stages 2 and 3*
Leicestershire Constabulary, Network
Educational Press
www.networkpress.co.uk

Tools for Tackling Racism in Schools
Stella Dadzie, Trentham Books, 1999

Values for Thinking
Robert Fisher, Nash Pollock 1997
ISBN 1898255377

The Whisperer
Nick Butterworth, Harper Collins, 2004

*Not Now Bernard, The Very Hungry
Caterpillar* and *The Great Big Enormous
Turnip*
from http://www.rdsbooks.com/ or
http://www.mantralingua.com/